Graphic Design: America Two

ROCKPORT

Graphic Design: America Two

Portfolios from the Best and Brightest Design Firms from Across the United States

Introduction by
Veronique Vienne

Organized by DK Holland,
Jessica Helfand, Chip Kidd
Produced by
The Pushpin Group

Visual Essays by
Sam Silvio (Chicago),
Susan Silton (Los Angeles),
Gary Keopke (Portland) and
Peter Good (Connecticut)

Published by
Rockport/Allworth Editions
Rockport Publishers, Inc.
Allworth Press

R|A

First published in the United States by Rockport/Allworth
Editions, a trade name of Rockport Publishers, Inc. and
Allworth Press

Rockport Publishers, Inc.
33 Commercial Street
Gloucester, Massachusetts 01930
Telephone: 978-282-9590
Facsimile: 978-283-2742
www.rockpub.com

Allworth Press
10 East 23rd Street
New York, NY 10010
Telephone: 212-777-8395
Facsimile: 212-777-8261

ISBN 1-56496-681-x
Printed in China

Table of Contents

Acknowledgements

It was Tad Crawford of Allworth Press who conceived the idea of a series of books about the work of graphic designers. The first book, published in 1992, is titled *Graphic Design: New York—The Work of 39 Great Graphic Design Firms from the City That Put Graphic Design on the Map* (volume two is also coming out this year).

GDNY's success created such a high visibility for graphic design that it led us to conceive *Graphic Design: America—The Work of Twenty-eight Design Firms from Across the United States and Canada,* and now the second volume, *Graphic Design: America Two—Portfolios from the Best and Brightest Firms from Across the United States.* Others are: *Signs and Spaces—A Survey of the Environmental Graphic Design Work of Twenty-two Major International Design Firms* and *Design in Depth—Unique Projects Created, Visually Explored and Analyzed by Fifty-one Leading Design Firms.* Of course the next natural step was the need to educate the world about illustration, so we created *Illustration: America—Outstanding Portfolios,* which was published in 1996.

Tad had the vision to include Rockport Publishers as co-publishers of the book. Rockport Publishers' Stan Patey and Arthur Furst lent their invaluable publishing and sales expertise and wisdom throughout the project.

Thank you to Scott Gilbertson, who assisted with the book's initial design processes, and Matt Verssue: both helped to contact the design firms in the beginning when they were students at the University of Kansas. Janet Shaeffer and Patty Swinney, also of KU, devoted many hours working on the organizational aspects of the book.

A special thank you to Julie Hillemeyer and Rebecca Horowitz. Julie and Rebecca started on the book while students of the University of Kansas and continued on at Pushpin to complete the project after graduation. Julie was the primary designer of the entire book. She reworked the grid and style from the first volume to both update and better display all the firms' work. During the final process, Julie brought the book back to her hometown of St. Louis and, working under a tight deadline, finished the color-proofing process with a dedication that is unmatched. Rebecca Horowitz copy edited this book, creating the style and controlling its content. Julie and Rebecca coordinated and kept track of all the firms throughout the design of the book, as well as completed its production: They put in countless hours, nights and weekends in a tireless team effort geared towards achieving the best book possible.

Dedication

alter Landor was a graphic designer, a gentleman and damn-good business man. He founded and built what is often referred to as the largest design firm in the world. And although he had high degree of authority and power in the design world, in a way, Walter didn't start a business, he embraced a profession. Designers were his friends and colleagues, not his competitors. He saw design as a practical business tool to help communicate a message to the consumer while creating a powerful, high-quality design—concerning himself with the needs of the consumer, not just the needs of the designer.

This book is dedicated to the memory of a generous man, who was also a visionary in the profession of graphic design: Walter Landor, Chief Executive Officer of Landor Associates, San Francisco.

DK Holland
New York

About This Book

Graphic Design: America, volume one, was approached with a spirit of celebration by Michael Beirut, William Drenttel and myself. We had just completed Graphic Design: New York and, having done so, felt it was high time to spread the good word about our nation's designers and their work.

Graphic Design: America was compiled by gathering all the great design firms and designers from around the country. An important goal was to highlight emerging talent and so we discovered designers in the process that had not become household names. This thrilled us and made the book more exciting, and we found designers from all the major cities.

Now, from the desire to continue to showcase new talent comes Graphic Design: America Two, organized by Jessica Helfand, Chip Kidd and myself. Realizing the country's vastness, I spent a year researching all 50 states, mainly from contacts made through the American Institute of Graphic Arts chapters. Of course, we also knew of individuals who we wished to invite into the book, but without the AIGA chapter's collective ear to the ground in the geographic areas, we would have missed many of the newest designers.

One note about this second volume: Jessica, Chip and I decided right off that this book was a clean slate. So many new designers had emerged in the few years between the two volumes, that most design firms from the first book had to give way to newer talent. William Drenttel had

predicted three years ago, when we first addressed the idea of a second volume, that many designers would be working in interactive media. This was a revolutionary concept at the time. Would designers really turn from the print medium to create digital design? In the midst of finishing the second volume, I realized that most firms had embraced digital media and were well involved with cyberspace, so we decided to include their website addresses. The Internet is so new to us— yet a market has opened creating interesting new challenges for design as a field, in professional practice and in the development of the client/ designer relationship.

While deciding who to choose as the participants for this book, one more goal was clear: We must express the range of designers across our nation today. We went to great lengths to display the gamut—from individual creators to large design firms representing, in all cases, the best and the brightest talent of the United States of America today.

DK Holland
New York

Back to the Frontier

Most Europeans—this writer included—look up to American culture with a mixture of awe and anguish. When asked what it is exactly that they love—and hate—about it, they make a face, bite their lips, cross their arms on their chest and look down at their shoes. They won't tell. No, it's not something about Hemingway, Mailer or Woody Allen. They have no problem with Dylan, Presley or Madonna. They have adopted The Honeymooners, I Love Lucy and Star Trek reruns as their own. So, what is it? The truth is apparently too embarrassing for words. Trying to get even the most enthusiastic Americanophile to describe what's so compelling about this culture is like trying to nail Jell-O to a wall.

You said Jell-O? I guess that's it. Like the American culture, Jell-O is artificial, but it wiggles, it dances, it's on the loose; it's self-evident, yet it escapes definition as surely as it escapes from your fingers if you try to pick it up. Most important, Jell-O is something you didn't know you wanted until you realized that life wasn't quite complete without it. Jell-O is what's right and what's wrong with this country. Jell-O is pure gelatin and food coloring—and pure marketing.

Who would have guessed that, as the dust settles at the end of this American century, marketing—not literature, pop music or even Hollywood—would emerge as the defining medium for this entire nation. Today, the real American folk heroes (or villains) are not the John Waynes or the Liz Taylors of the silver screen, but the Nike ads, the Coke commercials, Calvin Klein Barbies and The Gap T-shirts that are so popular here and abroad. As far as the world at large is concerned, that's what this country is all about. Not people, but logos. Not principles, but trademarks. Not democracy—brands.

The one thing Americans understand better than anyone else on this planet is how to create desires. Just flip through the pages of this book and look at the pictures—you don't need to know what they are, what they mean or what they are trying to say to feel their tug for your attention. Something urgent is going on, and you want to be part of it. This is marketing at its best. And there is nothing wrong with that—on the contrary. In *The Americans: The Democratic Experience*, author Daniel Boorstin tells how, in this country, the development of commercial trademarks has helped create a coherent American culture by giving immigrants who had nothing in common a shared medium. He notes that brand names "drew together in novel ways people who might not otherwise have been drawn together at all…. The particular importance of American consumption communities made it easier to assimilate, to 'Americanize' the millions who arrived here since the Civil War."

One of the designers featured in this book, Sonia Greteman from the Greteman Group, in Witchita, Kansas, says it best: "Ours is a combination of intuitive design solutions and the prairie's purple skies and amber waves," she writes

Milton Young and his wife, Helen, in his studio in Fresno, CA, circa 1927. Proud to be called a commercial artist, Young had a small and busy design practice. A painter, a letterer and a photo-retoucher, he could do by hand the work now performed by software programs like Illustrator, Fontographer and Photoshop. Otherwise, he was no different from so many graphic design professionals today: he designed whatever had to be designed for his community.

in her introduction. "Rooted in the spirit of the grassland, the past and the present are explored and an adventurous attitude is evident." Marc English, from Austin, Texas, shares this sort of thinking when he states that he feels "equally comfortable with clients of commerce and culture," and that his vocabulary is "steeped in history & story; Modernism & vernacular; precision and punk." There seems to be plenty of room for design pioneering between the covers of this book. "I think our work is most effective when it evokes a disturbing beauty," says Richard Smith from Firehouse 101 Art + Design, in Columbus, Ohio. "By disturbing I mean the quality to peel back an additional layer of obviousness to invite human emotions into the communication process."

The surprise is that, in this so-called materialistic country, goods are a lot less important than the emotions they provoke and the imagery they evoke. Marketing means selling hope in a bottle, they say. More often than not, that bottle bears one of many big-brand labels: Levi's, Disney, Nike, Coke, Seagram's, Ford, Apple, you name it. But, as we all know, ultimately, a bottle must be recycled. What counts is its flammable content. "The identity of an institution is no different from that of a person," says Rebeca Méndez from South Pasadena, California. "Some components remain static, like a backbone, but identity should be dynamic, continually evolving."

The best brands are living entities, indeed. Take Levi's, for example. It was 20 years in the making before receiving a patent in 1873. Levi Strauss, an immigrant from Bavaria, began selling denim jeans in the 1850s in California during the Gold Rush. What made his pants different at first was the fabric, a sturdy imported twill. In 1860, he added the rivets. But it's only in 1873 that he put the final touch on his product: a double arc stitched on the back pockets with orange thread. Only then did it all come together. Only then did Levi Strauss & Co become a brand.

Most American brands would make great copy—their stories ready to be optioned for movies. The Camel logo, for example, was drawn from a photograph of a Barnum & Bailey dromedary taken when the circus happened to pass through Winston-Salem in 1913. During the photo shoot, "Old Joe," as the beast was called, wouldn't keep still, so his trainer hit him on the nose—thus the outraged look and the raised tail of the now famous camel.

All those powerful supermarket brands started quite innocently. Band-Aid came about when the young wife of a Johnson & Johnson employee kept burning her fingers on her kitchen stove. The Gerber Baby was born in Fremont, Michigan, in 1928, a couple of months after Dan Gerber's own baby was switched to solid food. Ivory Soap was a gift from Heaven: Harley Procter, of Procter and Gamble fame, was sitting in church listening to the minister's sermon one Sunday in 1878, trying to come up with a name for his new white soap, the one that's "so pure, it floats," when he heard the preacher's words: "Out of the ivory palaces... whereby they have made thee glad." America's most popular soap was named after Psalms 45:8.

Graphic designers today are rediscovering the importance of the vernacular and the endemic when creating enduring visual communication. To transcend what Allemann Almquist & Jones from Philadelphia call "come-and-go design fads," they are renewing the great American tradition of individualism. "Come up with colorful, funny, provocative, in-your-face, on-the money, can't-ignore-it, hocus-pocus answers to the same questions," write Robynne Raye and Michael Strassburger from Modern Dog in Seattle. "Do it for bigwigs like Nike and Showtime. Do it for the art gallery that's opening two blocks down, or for the Northwest AIDS Foundation. Do it for your cousin Joe—it doesn't matter. What does matter is that you are having a great time."

Susan Silton, principal of SoS, Los Angeles, takes a different approach. A renowned artist and graphic designer, she chose not to promote her studio in this book. Instead, she created an art piece expressing her concerns with the design field's indifference to non-mainstream points of view. Her series of romanticized landscapes on page 210 are studio backdrops with imbedded text—a commentary on what we call "Natural." "In representing faux nature, I remind viewers that all ideas about nature are constructed and socially mediated. If nature is constructed, then one can adopt one's place in it," she says. "I link this to gay and lesbian identity, which is indefatigably attacked for being 'unnatural.'"

Graphic designers in America have always had to invent a place for themselves—if not in "nature" as defined by Silton, at least in the world of business. Their role was never taken for granted. "In the West, everything had to be developed, invented, when it was settled," says DK Holland, who co-edited this book. "My grandfather, E.L. Holland, was what was then simply called an 'artist' in Omaha, Nebraska, where he settled from London, a penniless immigrant." As a landscape painter and a writer, E.L. was a natural visual communicator. He came to the new city of Omaha loaded with his paintings and drawings. He worked as a commercial artist eventually started an advertising agency that later became one of the largest in the Midwest, Rollheiser Holland Kahler. But most of E.L.'s clients were regional retail accounts: the local furniture store, the local men's clothing establishment, for whom he created billboards, advertising and catalogs. "The success of his business was due to the fact that all his work had a clear sense of purpose," notes Holland. "Clarity of image and word combined with taste and art: E.L. could really put it all together."

My husband's father, Milton Young, was part of the same tradition. Born in Riverside, California and raised in Fresno, he was a gifted painter and a self-taught letterer. Back then, people were proud to be called commercial artists. Like so many professionals whose work is displayed in the following pages, Milton Young had a small agency—but it supported him and his

far left
Milton Young's landscape,
painted in the 1940s,
expressed his love of Nature.

left
Susan Silton's conceptual
piece, on the other hand,
expresses how society's idea
of what is natural is co-opted
and mediated.

family comfortably for decades—between 1919, when he came back from World War I at age 18, to 1963, when he died three months after retiring. Like the folks at Modern Dog, he designed whatever had to be designed for his local community: labels for fruit crates, billboards for the Chamber of Commerce and ads in the local papers. His two big clients were Sun Maid Raisin (he came up with the original logo) and, during World War II, the Air Force, which kept him busy with aerial maps. His real passion was landscape painting, though. He never thought the pictures he painted were conceptual pieces—but, as do E.L. Holland's, they look a lot like Susan Silton's backdrops.

The stories we could tell about the lives of the people who create our graphic communication! Their personal experience is so much part of the language they share with us. Aware of the powerful impact of the anecdotal—and no longer concerned about sounding "professional"—more and more graphic designers are deliberately incorporating odd biographical details into their firm's mission statement. "Communication that doesn't take a change doesn't stand a chance," remarks Carlos Segura, creator of a Chicago digital type foundry [T-26] and principal of Segura Inc.

It's a big extended design family out there. Jack and Jeff Gernsheimer from Partners Design, Inc. in Bernville, Pennsylvania, are identical twins. The brothers "attribute much of their success to their exceptional closeness." At Cummings & Good in Chester, Connecticut, Peter Good and Janet Cummings make no bones about their sharing "the tenacity to have survived (mostly gracefully) three decades of collaborating in art, marriage, parenting and business." In Bloomfield Hills, Michigan, Scott Makela and soulmate Laurie Haycock Makela of Words + Pictures for Business + Culture explain that, as a married couple, they "go out of their way to invade boundaries and twist the rules."

American graphic designers reach beyond the conventional because, in the words of Jeffrey Morris from Studio Morris in New York, the best design firms combine "both an intuitive and a rational approach." If anything, computers are helping designers meld emotion with thoughts, art with commerce and personal vision with universal communication. Instead of fast-forwarding into a digitalized, cognitively-correct future, the technology is encouraging people to embrace a this-is-my-life approach to their craft.

Recently, a friend of mine mentioned that he was flying down to Miami on PanAm. "You aren't flying on PanAm," I said, "you are flying in an airplane with the old PanAm logo painted on its tail. Don't be fooled: a small airline just bought the right to use the logo." I felt smug, but the look of chagrin on his face made me wish I had kept my mouth shut. In this day and age, you don't belittle someone's brand. It's like denigrating his or her family values, belief system and aesthetic judgment. Instead, you celebrate the language of trade—and keep trading ideas.

Veronique Vienne
Brooklyn, New York

When graphic designers were first and foremost illustrators and painters:

left
Billboard for Del Monte Catsup. Designer and date are unknown.

left
Billboard advertising Fresno's commerce. Designer, Milton Young.

middle and bottom
Two billboards: Westinghouse Battery and Sutro Baths and Museum. Designers or dates unknown.

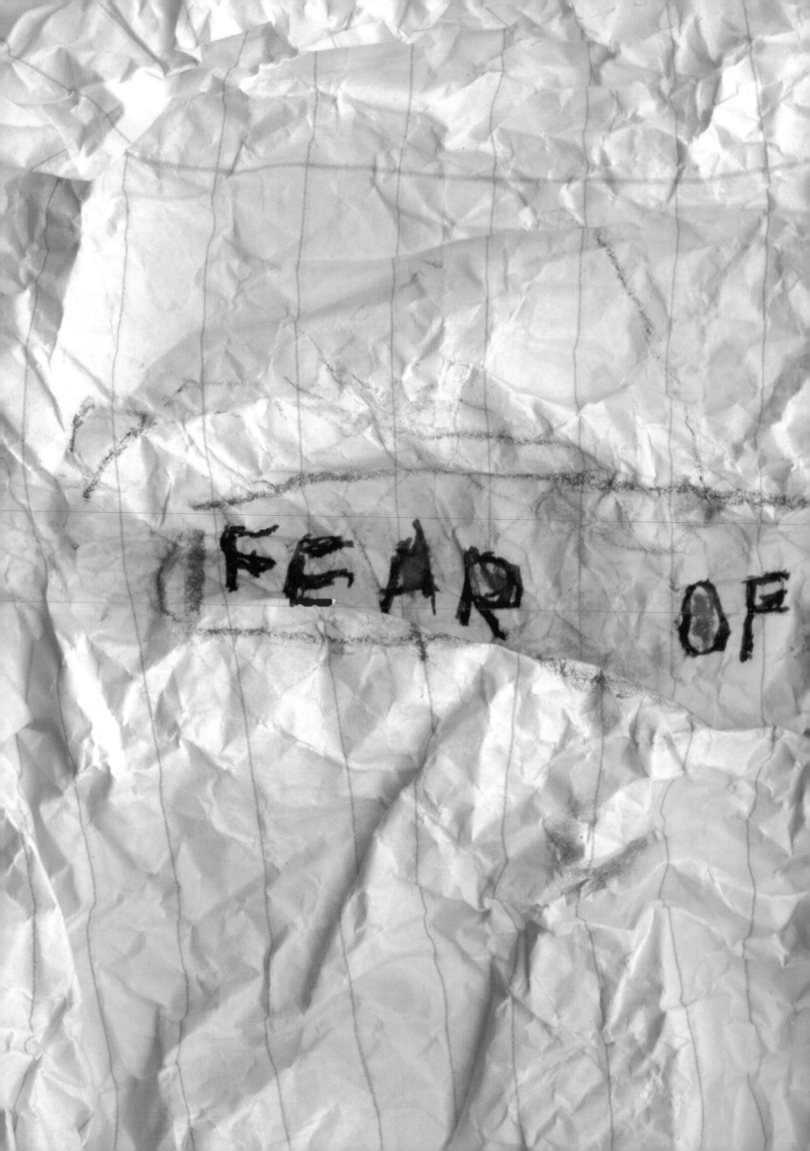

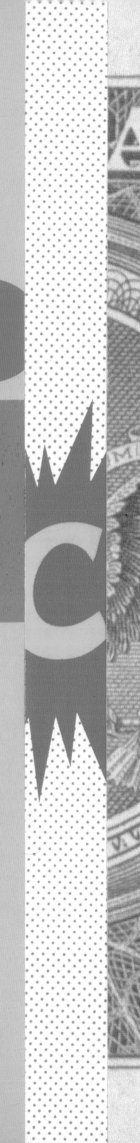

arrivals from Europe ar
and desirable Goods, su
of which are of their own
reat care, all of which t
tock consists in part of t
and American Broadcl
milled, in black, blues
from common to extra fin
blues, &c. plain, diam
Cassimeres and Doeskins,
erman blk Doeskins; Ve
styles, in rich Cashmer
yons silk Velvets; do, wi
nd Alpacca Serges; Canv
s; brown Hollands; Buf
s and Vest Cords and Bind
Cloak Linings; 6-4 Silk V
aid do; Orleans Cloths, i
stripe, plaid and change
, new patterns; rich new
Cashmere d'Ecosse; Mou
ines; Chusans; rich Cl
Furnitures; colored Cam
nd Muslins, plain, strip
Worsted and Linen Da
coman's Cravats, a great
Braces, all qualities; F
ravats; Plaid do; fancy S
ongee and other Hdkfs; a
and Lamb's Wool Shirts
nd white Flannels, 3-4
g; Scotch Diaper and C
astings, plain and figure
do Damasks, in worsted
, and green; Worsted P
Velveteen; black and fa
se Blankets; Horse do,
Burlaps; black, white
histle Spool Cotton, wh
do do Lacets; best solid
& Eyes; bleached, half
nd twill'd; together with
Goods, such as brown an
; Drills; Jeans; striped

LL AND WINT
d Country Trade, by
RLES A. WHITE & CO.
ceived, and are now ope
te assortment of season
which they offer for sale
rns, and at the very lowe
, CASSIMERES, VESTING
Goods, as follows:
DCLOTHS—Superlative Fr
olives, browns, and other
sh; medium and low qua
or.
AMERICAN CLOTHS, of th
ors.
above Cloths are plain
uble milled, for surtouts.
MERES—English, French
n great variety.
KINS—Blacks and fancy
le, from the highest to th
ER CLOTHS—Black, blue
OR CLOTHS—Black, blue,
erican manufacture.
CLOTHS—English, Germ
ors.
NGS—A very extensive
able styles of French and
ET VESTINGS—In every st
atin Vestings, of the new
re, Woollen Velvet, Vale
VELVETS—Blue and jet
ent.
SERGES—Extra heavy, fi
ccas—Superior Silk War
NA and ALPACCA SERGES
DS—In all styles of plain,
KINGS—Of the newest pat
LLEN LININGS—A com
for all descriptions of wi
ON FLANNEL LININGS—D
g SILK—Rogers' best Na
ings—Silk, Worsted and
d Overcoat and Vest Cord
ONS—Of every description
HALL'S THREAD—All num
lnshings;

LVETS, SATINS
perior and medium L
do do Serges; best Itali
the package or piece, by

RMAN WOOLEN
CO. have in store, ju
es German Castor BEAV
do Doeskin do;
do Twilled Surtou
do 6-4 and 3-4 DO
do Plain and Twi
ved, per Florida, (via Ne
piece or package, at No.

RNSWORTH &
reet, offer for sale th
oods, viz:
ancy Cashmere de Ecosse
urning do do;
per Fancy Coreans;
Worsted Bohemians;
nd Fancy Crape de Paris;
ancy Taizans;
Warp Alpaccas;
black Janmisse;
ack Orleans and Alpacca
oyal blue do;

R CALEDONIA.
res; 3 do Mouslin de
o colored Indianas; I do
riss Mulls; I do Bishop L
ambrics; I do white and c
oods—for sale by LITTL
Congress streets.

O. H. LEMIST
Milk street, have rece
es British Dry Goods, a
r sale—consisting in part
lk, blk and col'd Cloths;
d fancy Doeskins;
mill'd Cassimeres;
nd medium fancy Vestin
lk and blue Beavers;
lnshings;
blue Beavers;

Adams Morioka, Inc.

Principal: Sean Adams,
Noreen Morioka
Year Founded: 1994
Size of Firm: 5
Key Clients: A+M Records,
Barton Myers Associates,
Inc., DMJM Architecture,
Eli Broad Foundation,
Ellerbe Becket Architects,
LA Louver Gallery,
Pacific Design Center,
The Ahmanson Theater,
The Getty Center for the
History of Art and
Humanities, Universal/
MCA, Wired Magazine.

2011 Pontius Avenue
Los Angeles, CA 90025
310 477 4227

(at press time, a merger with
Maddocks & Company has
been completed)

dams/Morioka's commitment to clearing away the tricks and "40,000 boxes"—paring communication down to its most direct and thoughtful level—is counterpointed by the firm's reputation as the "friendly alternative." The collaboration between the two principals, Sean Adams and Noreen Morioka, and the chemistry with their clients spurred one to contend, "Can you say Adams/Morioka without a smile?" At the core of the philosophy supporting the firm is clarity of message, purity of form, and resonance in meaning. These concepts, along with the idea of the "virtual office," help Adams/ Morioka to create corporate identity programs for multi-national corporations, video, web sites, large scale environmental graphics, packaging—and most recently, a full-length gown.

left
Poster promoting the work of Ed Moses and Tony Berlant at the recently completed LA Louver Gallery, Venice, CA. Because the openings occurred on separate dates the poster was created topsy-turvy, allowing the person hanging the piece to determine which event took priority.
Photography, Brian Forrest.

above
Poster announcing the Southern California Institute of Architecture's Spring Lecture Series. A grouping of narrative images that promoted ideas of Spring allowed its viewers to make their own conclusions.

left
Sean Adams and
Noreen Morioka.
Photography, Photomaton
Bon Marché.

below left and below
Interior and exterior banners
and changeable signage for
the Pacific Design Center.
To allow the Center to speak
to the public, the messages
are relayed simply and in four
languages wherever possible.

below
Poster and promotional
materials for the Pacific
Design Center, Los Angeles,
CA. The globe is an interchangeable grid of images.
The images within the
globe changed depending
upon the application. This
particular event took place
soon after the LA riots, fires
and Northridge earthquake,
so all the materials tried to
incorporate ideas of safety,
security and confidence.

パシフィック デザイン センター

太平洋設計中心

Centro de Diseño del Pacífico
Pacific Design Center

right
Book about architecture and
gender, for William Morrow
Publishers, New York, NY.
The book utilizes a language
related to pornography and
scholarly texts. The book
was a promotion in itself due
to its obvious and subversive
display opportunities.
Designers, Sean Adams,
Noreen Morioka and
Richard Shanks.

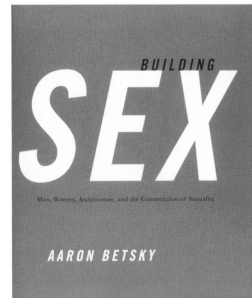

BUILDING
SEX

Men, Women, Architecture, and the Construction of Sexuality

AARON BETSKY

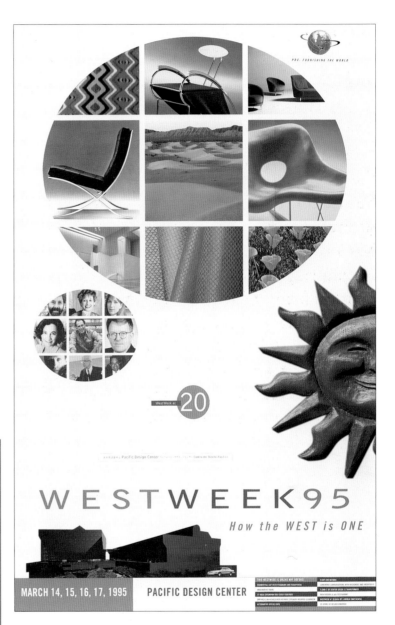

WESTWEEK95
How the WEST is ONE

MARCH 14, 15, 16, 17, 1995   PACIFIC DESIGN CENTER

left and below

Magazine advertisement about a fundraising benefit and fashion show for the AIDS Project, Los Angeles, CA. A full-length pink taffeta madras gown was designed specifically for the fashion show.

below right

Poster announcing a lecture series with non-architects, for The Lost Angeles Forum for Architecture and Urban Design. The poster utilized natural images in a rigid, modernist environment to promote lectures given by a poet, a furniture maker, an art critic and a light artist.

totally cupid

a valentine's tribute to love and fashion

left

Poster and invitation announcing an exhibition of political posters. Previously banned in Kansas City, MO, the slogan, "Don't Be A Sheep" was used in response to the controversy. The product was printed on cheap newsletter paper, mailed and illegally "spliced" onto construction site walls.

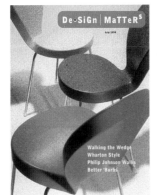

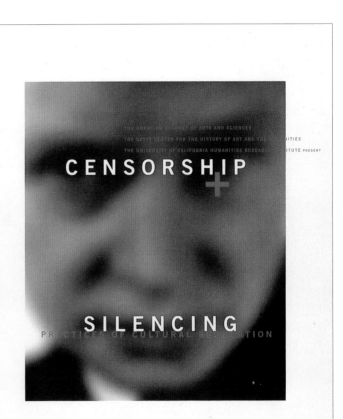

left
A proposed layout for a new magazine, *Design Matters*, New York, NY. To appeal to a large audience, the pages were designed in an aesthetically pleasing, classic format, but was slightly skewed with color and typographic choices.

left
Advertisement announcing the arrival of film and video director, Jonathan Taylor, at See Company, Santa Monica, CA. Over 200 phone calls in direct response from the ad were made on the day of its release. Photography, Jonathan Taylor.

right
Poster for The Getty Center for the History of Art and the Humanities, Los Angeles, CA. The poster announced a year-long series of lectures about issues of expression and repression. Each lecture was held in a different city to accommodate a conglomerated audience.

left
Call for entries poster for the 1994 Annual Design Awards, sponsored by the American Institute Architecture, Los Angeles, CA. No specific architecture was used to avoid heavily promoting a specific style. Alternatively, the imagery focused on people and their lives within architecture.

bottom row
Graphic identities, interior signage, architecture, materials and color palettes for IdeaHouse at the Pacific Design Center, Los Angeles, CA. The 25,000-square-foot renovation provided space for emerging talent in furniture, textiles and industrial design. Designers, Sean Adams, Noreen Morioka and Richard Shanks.

right and below
Sign system and color palette for the Music Center Group, Los Angeles, CA. It was an important criteria to create a signage system for the Ahmanson theater that was classic and pure rather than trendy and decorative—hence the subdued color palette and legible typographic system.
Art Directors, Sean Adams and Noreen Morioka; designers, Adams, John Guard and Richard Shanks, Ellerbe Becket, Architects.

opposite page/first row
Visual identity for Edge Television, Los Angeles, CA. The new network's programming involved experimental film and video with an emphasis on cutting edge.

opposite page/second row
Video for A+M Records, Los Angeles, CA. The 30-minute video previewed the label's selected artists, and was shown at the annual NARM Convention, and then shipped to record stores and distributors. Rather than using a live action host, graphics and a visual vocabulary acted as the host for all artists.
Art Director/Designers, Sean Adams and Noreen Morioka; directors, Jonathan Dayton and Valerie Faris.

ideahouse

opposite page/sixth row
"Cyberbia" interactive television series for Maverick Television, Los Angeles, CA. A systems manual of functions, placement and appearance timing of the animated icons was created for consistency.
Art Directors/Designers, Sean Adams and Noreen Morioka; director/producer, Dayton Faris.

third and fourth row
Titles, interstitial graphics and short piece title graphics in "The Works" television series for PBS/KCET, Los Angeles, CA. The three-part series consisted of 22 experimental film and video projects from a variety of artists and topics. The on-line graphics served to create continuity and linkage of the individual pieces.

fifth row
Titles and image/text sequences for REM's Monster Tour Documentary, Athens Ltd., Athens, GA. Based on "incorrect" timing and vocabulary of typographic elements and icons, the typography interacted with sound and images in a seemingly haphazard fashion. Art Director/Designers, Sean Adams and Noreen Morioka; directors, Jonathan Dayton and Valerie Faris.

Greater Valley Medical Group, Inc.

left
Corporate identity for Greater Valley Medical Group, Los Angeles, CA. The identity program harnessed all three hospitals and most offices into a cohesive whole, focusing on health, confidence and a sense of welcome.

Allemann Almquist & Jones

Principals:
Hans-U Allemann,
Jan C. Almquist
Year Founded: 1984
Size of Firm: 7
Key Clients: Bell Atlantic,
The Children's Hospital of
Philadelphia, CIGNA
Corporation, The Fairmount
Park Art Association,
The Franklin Institute
Science Museum,
Hercules, Inc.; J.P. Morgan,
Maritrans, Inc.;

PHH Corporation,
Saint Joseph's University,
Villanova University,
WHYY Wilmington/
Philadelphia.

301 Cherry Street
3rd Floor
Philadelphia, PA 19106-1803
215 829 9442

Allemann Almquist & Jones collectively share a high standard of integrity, quality and discipline. A passion to create and mutual respect drew the founding partners, Hans-U. Allemann, Jan C. Almquist and Dana J. Jones together in 1984. These same qualities remain the foundations of the studio today, which has grown to include seven designers. Fluent in photography, illustration and typography, the craftsmen and artists have created the AA&J style—transcending come-and-go design fads—remaining fresh and appealing, even in retrospect. Its work, which includes corporate identity, corporate and institutional marketing and annual report design, seeks to communicate the client's message unequivocally, while satisfying the visual appetite. It is a synthesis of strategic planning, problem solving and visual thinking.

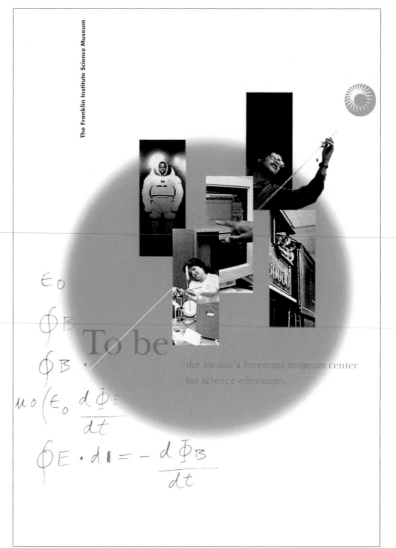

above
Brochure cover for the Franklin Institute's Strategic Plan, Philadelphia, PA. It highlights the various constituencies that the Institute serves.
Designer, Jan C. Almquist.

left
Identity for The Franklin Institute Science Museum, an institution dedicated to museum-based science education as a means of increasing public understanding of science and its relevance to our future.
Designer, Hans-U. Allemann.

left
Hans-U. Allemann and
Jan C. Almquist.

above
Brochure cover for the
Children's Hospital of
Philadelphia, PA, produced
to raise money for a new
research facility.
Art Director, Hans-U.
Allemann; designers,
Allemann and
Gregory Paone.

left
Poster for The Hagley
Museum and Library,
Wilmington, DE. It adver-
tises a series of symposia
about industry's impact on
the environment.
Design/Photography,
Jan C. Almquist.

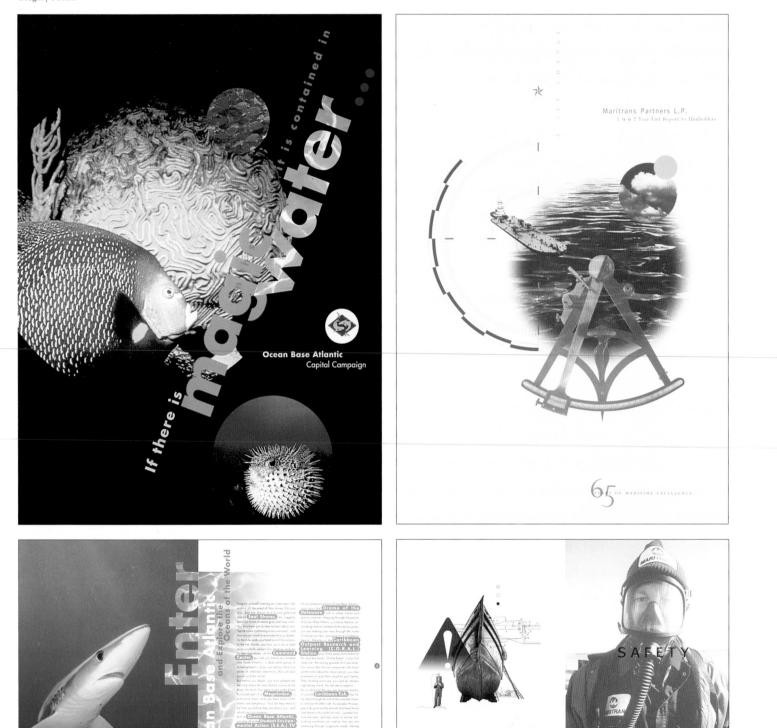

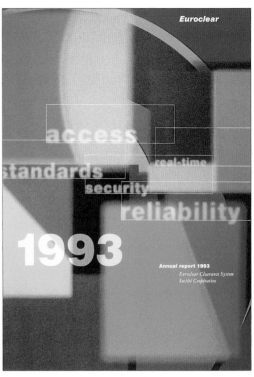

left and above
Annual report for Euroclear
Clearance System Société
Coopérative, Brussels,
Belgium. The cover and
inside image from the 1993
annual report highlights
areas of technological
expertise through bold
iconographic imagery
and typography.
Art Director, Jan C.
Almquist; designers,
Almquist and
Stephen Shackleford;
photography, Almquist.

Identity for the Institute for
Science Information (ISI)
Science Citation Index,
compact disk edition,
Philadelphia, PA.
Art Director, Hans-U.
Allemann, designers,
Allemann and Mark James.

Identity for Abbey Camera,
Philadelphia, PA.
Designer, Jan C. Almquist.

Identity for Savings & Loan
Bank, Solothurn,
Switzerland, specializing
in home mortgages.
Designer,
Hans-U. Allemann.

Identity for Order of St.
Augustine, Villanova, PA,
celebrating its 200th-U.S.
anniversary with the theme,
"Sharing the Fire."
Designers,
Stephen Shackleford,
Hans-U. Allemann and
Jan C. Almquist.

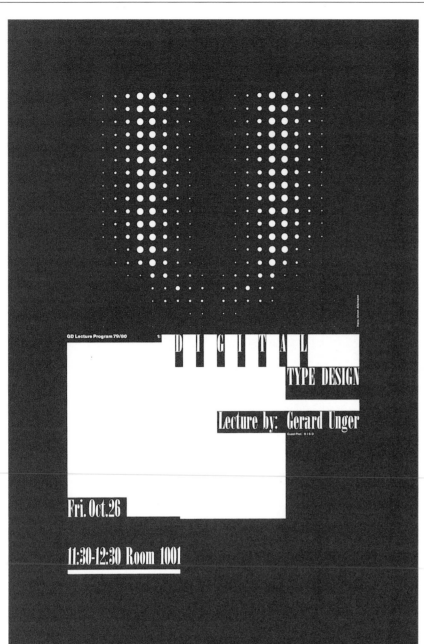

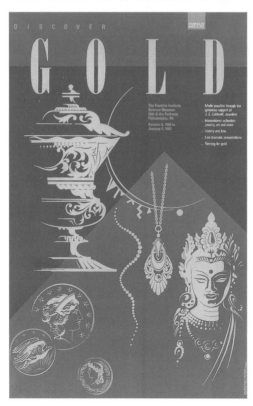

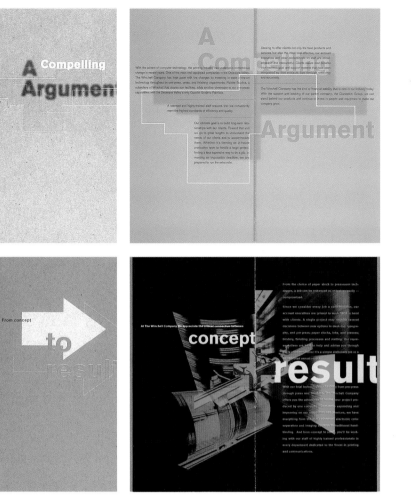

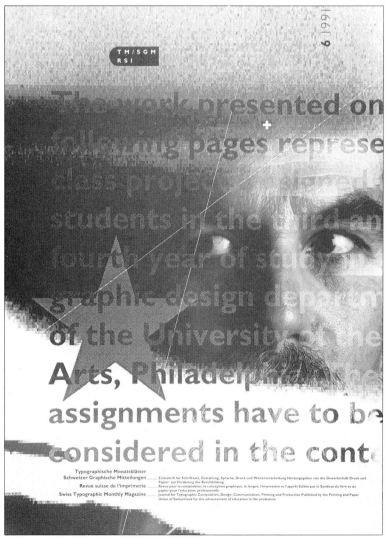

above
Covers and spreads from
"A Compelling Argument"
and "Concept to Result,"
two pieces in a serial-mailing
for The Winchell Company,
Philadelphia, PA, a printer
addressing the sensitivity on
issues of printing excellence.
Art Directors, Hans-U.
Allemann and Jan C.
Almquist; designers, Almquist
and Stephen Shackleford.

right
Cover for Typographische
Monatsblätter Magazine,
Switzerland. The issue con-
tains a feature article on
Hans-U. Allemann's com-
munications class curriculae
at the University of the Arts.
Design/Photography,
Jan C. Almquist.

Asher Studio

Principal: Connie Asher
Year Founded: 1977
Size of Firm: 4
Key Clients: Boulder
Community Hospital,
The Centennial Funds,
Cheley Colorado Camps,
Hewlett-Packard, Kaiser
Permanente, Mile High
United Way, National
Jewish, Norwest Banks,
Pharmacy Corporation of
America, Security Life,
Sevo Miller, U S West.

1700 East 17th Avenue
Suite 200
Denver, CO 80218
303 321 5599

Asher Studio appreciates the value of synergy. When you look at a body of work produced by a design firm, it's easy to assume that everything reflects one designer's ideas. The reality is much more interesting. Good design comes from a team of independent thinkers who pull together with style, grace and humor under the pressure of real-world budgets, surprises and deadlines. And the team is extensive: designers, clients, writers, photographers, illustrators and printers who all care intensely about the effectiveness of the final product. "We find that real creativity feeds on the adrenaline that kicks in when good people work together in a spirit of adventure," says Connie Asher. "At Asher Studio, we believe in the power of a collaborative approach based on frank discussion and free-wheeling creativity with our client at the center of the process."

top right
Identity and collateral materials for Cortech, Inc., a Denver-based biopharmaceutical firm. The figure is a modern interpretation of the archetypal daVinci man. Designer, Connie Asher.

right
Healthcare enrollment packages for Kaiser Permanente, Denver, CO. A completely new system incorporating color coding and simplified language was created for the company's numerous health plans. Art Director, Connie Asher; designer, Katie McKenna; writer, Linda Cuyler; photography, Brad Bartholomew.

left
From left: Connie Asher,
Diane Graves and
Katie McKenna.
Photography,
Brad Bartholomew.

below
Brochure, 75th-anniversary
logo and postcard package
for Cheley Colorado Camps,
Estes Park, CO. The focus
is on details that bring
Cheley to life. Several layers
of information, including
historical drawings and
engravings from Cheley
archives, were woven
together to appeal to both
young people and parents.
Designers, Connie Asher,
Katie McKenna and Michael
Riggs; writer, Ginny Hoyle;
cover photography,
Dan Sidor.

SERVING BOYS AND GIRLS SINCE 1921

SEVENTY-FIVE SUMMERS

left to right
Chris McAllister
Illustration, Elysian, MN.
Designers, Connie Asher
and Michael Riggs.

LifeStory Software logo for
Pharmacy Corporation of
America, Wilsonville, OR.
Designer, Katie McKenna.

Unpublished.
Designer, Katie McKenna.

Rocky Mountain Rookie
League, Denver, CO.
Designer, Michael Riggs.

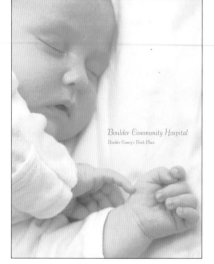

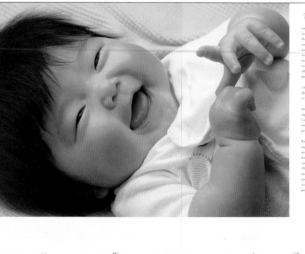

Marketing brochure for
obstetrical services, Boulder
Community Hospital,
Boulder, CO. Images of
babies—some larger than
life, with no parents or staff
in sight—enable prospective
parents to put themselves
into the moment.
Designers, Connie Asher
and Katie McKenna; writer,
Ginny Hoyle; illustrator,
Stephen Schudlich; photography, Brad Bartholomew.

head Over heels

elegance simplicity

truth clarity reality

creativity integrity

wonder sizzle

fun energy

insight trust logic

passion accuracy

commitment results

below
Identity and signage for
Sevo Miller, Denver, CO,
a commercial real estate
company. The strong vertical
form works in a wide range
of applications, helping it
to stand out in the highly-
competitive market.
Designers, Connie Asher
and Karey Christ-Janer.

above and below
Self-promotional Valentines,
an annual signature piece
for Asher Studio. The
Valentines give a "platform
to share the firm's beliefs
about life, design and
communication. This
assignment is pure pleasure."
Designers, Connie Asher,
Katie McKenna, Diane
Graves and Michael Riggs;
writer, Ginny Hoyle; illustrator, Connie Lehman.

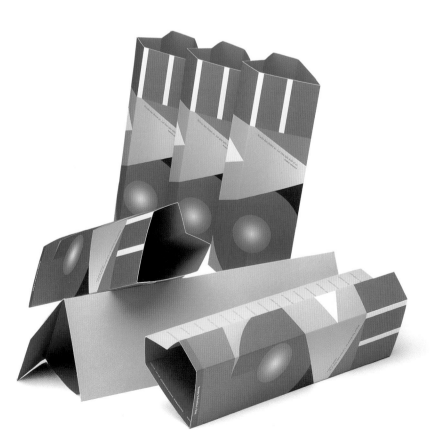

left
Sales kit for Security Life, Denver, CO. The Toolbox is a comprehensive sales product kit for insurance agents. The familiar name, tangible image and color coding system makes the package appealing and easy to use.
Designers, Connie Asher, Katie McKenna and Michael Riggs; illustrator, Matt Brownson; writers, Cindy Quinn, Georjean West and Ginny Hoyle.

left and below
Brochure for Pharmacy Corporation of America, Longmont, CO. Bold, bright colors and extreme images are used to create a compact, high-energy brochure.
Art Director, Connie Asher; designer, Katie McKenna; photography, Todd Droy; writer, Laura Holloway.

above
Reference materials for Hewlett-Packard's Intelligent Electronics sales representatives.
Art Director, Connie Asher; designer, Katie McKenna.

left
Poster for Hewlett-Packard, Denver, CO, inviting Intelligent Electronics system engineers to its high-tech training conferences.
Art Director, Connie Asher; designer, Katie McKenna; illustrator, Chris McKay; writers, Shirley Loring and Ginny Hoyle.

left and below
Annual report for The Children's Hospital, Denver, CO. The report avoided staged photos of physicians and medical facilities in favor of photos of the hospital's young patients who have serious illnesses.
Designers, Connie Asher and Martha Carroll; photography, Brad Bartholomew; writer, Karen Goodridge; illustrators, students from Stevens Elementary School.

right
Product brochures for fax services, U S West, Denver, CO. Warm, high-tech photos integrated with benefit statements and straight forward, jargon-free copy makes the collateral accessible and inviting.
Designers, Connie Asher and Katie McKenna; writer, Ginny Hoyle; photography, Todd Droy and Brad Bartholomew.

Bielenberg Design

Principal: John Bielenberg
Year Founded: 1990
Size of Firm: 5
Key Clients: Advent
Software, Animated
Images, Inc., Deja Shoe,
Fidelity Management Trust
Company, Hewlett Packard,
ITG Inc., Montgomery
Securities, NIKE, Santa
Clara University, Shearson
Lehman Advisors, The
State Bar of California,
Wells Fargo Nikko
Investment Advisors.

2004 8th Street
Suite D
Boulder, CO 80302
303 473 0757

421 Tehama Street
San Francisco, CA 94103
415 495 3371

Bielenberg Design is built upon the premise that the professional practice of graphic design is about engineering a connection between a message and an audience. A cerebral, concept-driven approach is the foundation for all work produced by the firm. In addition to solving client-initiated problems, John Bielenberg is interested in exposing inaccurate assumptions about graphic design. He said, "Just like an addict creates a lust for drugs or alcohol, the designer can develop a craving for the new, the visually compelling and the beautiful. The image can become an end in itself and the message buried in subservience to the graphic language."

above
?! Book, a commentary on waste and lack of content in graphic design, is the second piece in a continuing series of self-initiated/funded projects. A 100-page hard-bound book containing only one message—that it was printed on recycled paper. Designers, John Bielenberg and Allen Ashton.

left
Promotional poster, 4-feet by 6-feet, the first piece in the series. It addresses the need for introspection by the design profession. Designers, John Bielenberg and Allen Ashton; printer, Robb Murray.

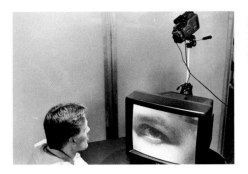

left
Left to right: John Bielenberg,
Mitsubishi Color Television
and JVC Camcorder.
Photography, Allen Ashton.

right and below
A parody annual report for
a fictitious company, Virtual
Telemetrix Inc., the third
piece in the series. The
project was originally
intended to trick designers
and competition judges by
producing a visually com-
pelling document that
communicated absolutely
nothing. However, the
report evolved into a piece
that pokes fun at the
designer, the annual report,
and corporate America.
Designers, John Bielenberg
and Allen Ashton;
contributors, Erik Adigard,
Dana Arnett, Michael
Cronan, Jilly Simons, Rick
Valicenti and John Watson.

VIRTUAL TELE METRIX 1993 ANNUAL REPORT

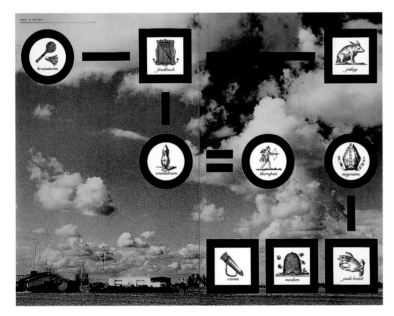

FINANCIAL
INFORMATION NOT
INTERESTING AT TIME
OF PUBLICATION.

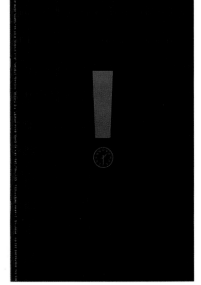

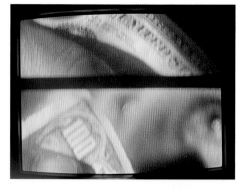

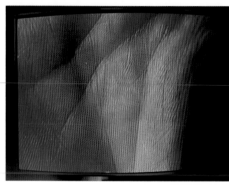

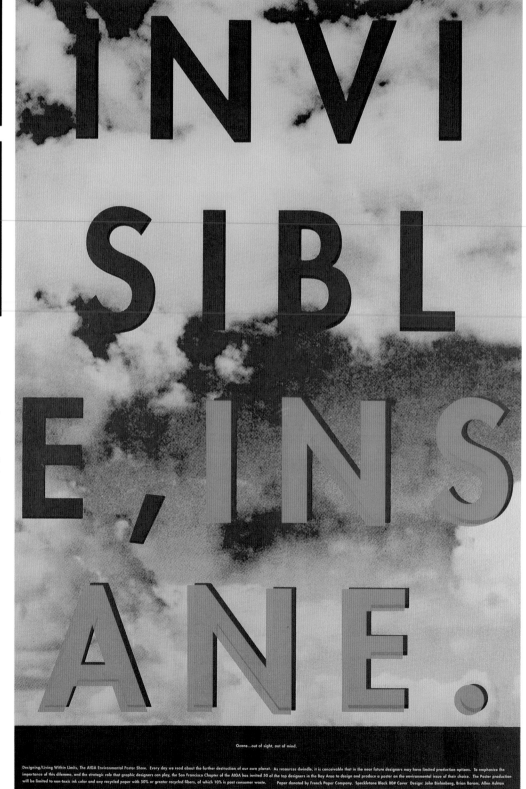

above
Deadly Sin identification
program for ID Magazine
Fantasy Portfolio, March
1991, New York, NY.
The objective was to create
colored symbols of the seven
deadly sins that would be
permanently impregnated
into the skin of a sinner.
"As greed replaces sex as the
vice of choice, the new scar-
let letter is 'A' for avarice."
Designers, John Bielenberg,
Allen Ashton and
Brian Boram; photography,
Paul Franz-Moore.

right
Poster for the American
Institute of Graphic Arts,
San Francisco, CA. The
poster, addressing ozone
erosion, was produced as
part of an exhibition of
posters focused on environmental issues. "Invisible,
insane" comes from a com-
puter that translated the
saying, "out of sight, out of
mind" from English to
Russian, and then back to
English.
Designers, John Bielenberg,
Allen Ashton and
Brian Boram;
photography, Ashton.

left
Centerpiece for the San Francisco Museum of Modern Art. Forty graphic designers, architects and interior designers were invited to design a table decoration for the Beaux Arts Ball, a fundraising event for the museum. For the theme, Bacchus, God of Wine, a liver was the centerpiece, napkins were held by surgical clamps and the serving plates were stainless steel specimen trays, all in an effort to inform about alcoholism and liver disease. "$1000 a plate dinner," Bielenberg said, "and you're staring at a liver on a stick."
Designers, John Bielenberg and Allen Ashton; fabricator, Brian Spitz.

below
Poster for Youth and Family Assistance, San Mateo, CA. Targeted at alienated and homeless teenagers, the poster gave information about where they could go for help.
Designers, John Bielenberg, Berndt Abeck and Allen Ashton; printer, Dharma Enterprises.

right
Poster for the Sexual Identity Forum, San Mateo, CA. The poster, aimed at gay, lesbian, bisexual, transgender and questioning high school students, announced a forum where gender issues could be openly discussed.
Designers, John Bielenberg, Allen Ashton and Teri Vasarhelyi; printer, Robb Murray.

IN EVERY CLASS, IN EVERY SCHOOL, IN EVERY CITY, IN EVERY STATE. GAY, LESBIAN, BISEXUAL, TRANSGENDER AND QUESTIONING YOUTH ARE EVERYWHERE. YOU COUNT. REACH OUT. GET SUPPORT.
THE SEXUAL IDENTITY FORUM IS A SAFE, SUPPORTIVE AND CONFIDENTIAL DROP IN GROUP FOR GAY, LESBIAN, BISEXUAL, TRANSGENDER AND QUESTIONING YOUTH IN SAN MATEO COUNTY. (415) 572-0535

left
Poster announcing a design seminar for the California College of Arts and Crafts, San Francisco, CA. The poster illustrates how the conceptual design process is like the struggle to climb a mountain. Bielenberg said, "There is a principle in physics that states: Systems tend to maintain a state of minimum energy and maximum disorder. It is the designer's job to combat these forces in the pursuit of the perfect conceptual solution."
Designers, John Bielenberg and Allen Ashton; photography, Marcel Ichac.

1. SYSTEMS TEND TO ATTAIN A STATE OF MINIMUM ENERGY
2. SYSTEMS TEND TOWARD A STATE OF MAXIMUM DISORDER

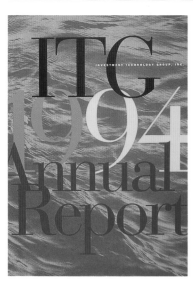

Annual report for Investment
Technology Group, Inc.,
New York, NY. This was
the first annual report for a
company that provides
computerized stock trading
services. Every spread, in
reaction against dense and
hard-to-access information,
has one key message pre-
sented as graphically large
as possible.
Designers, John Bielenberg
and Berndt Abeck; agency,
Dakin & Willison.

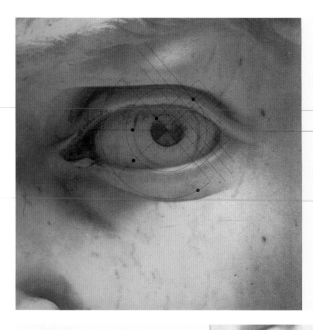

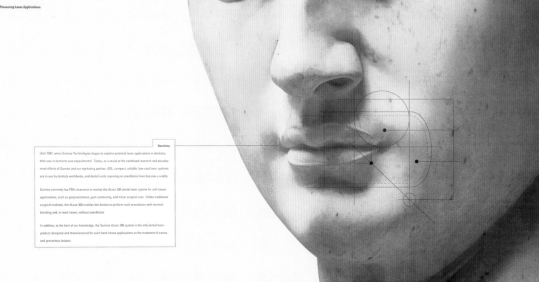

above
1991 annual report cover
design for Sunrise Tech-
nologies, Inc., Fremont,
CA, a company that makes
lasers for medical applications. Michelangelo's *David*
was used both as a symbol of
humanity and to position its
laser technology specifically
for medical applications.
Designers, John Bielenberg
and Allen Ashton; printer,
Dharma Enterprises.

left and above left
1990 annual report spreads
for Sunrise Technologies,
Inc. The photographs were
created by color copying
bland white photographs of
the statue and increasing
the color saturation to produce a DaVinci-like patina.
The color copies were then
scanned directly as art.
Designers, John Bielenberg,
Allen Ashton and Brian
Boram; printer, Lithographix.

right
Brochure for Bielenberg
Design and Communication
Arts Magazine, Palo Alto,
CA. The brochure explores
issues related to graphic
design practices in the service of communication. It
was reduced to the barest
minimum of graphic devices
to ensure that the only possible interest was in the
written content, not the
visual style.
Designer, John Bielenberg;
printer, Dharma Enterprises.

thinking about co mmunica tion.

above and right
Capabilities brochure for
Investment Advisors, Inc.,
Houston, TX. Each defining
investment principle of the
firm is connected to a season
and illustrated using trees
as metaphors—the firm has
endured and excelled during
the various "seasons" of the
financial markets.
Designers, John Bielenberg,
Allen Ashton and
Brian Boram; illustrator,
Rik Olson; agency,
Dakin & Willison.

SOLID *PHILOSOPHICAL ROOTS CARRY*
AN INVESTMENT MANAGER THROUGH
PERIODS WHEN THE MARKET ENVIRONMENTS
ARE UNSTABLE AND REACTIVE.

FLEXIBILITY AND
A COMPREHENSIVE PERSPECTIVE REVEAL
WAYS TO DEFEND AGAINST UNPRECEDENTED
MOVEMENT AND VOLATILITY

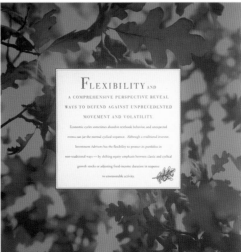

Cahan & Associates

Principal: Bill Cahan
Year Founded: 1984
Size of Firm: 15
Key Clients: Adaptec,
American First Financial
Corporation, Birkenstock,
COR Therapeutics,
Domaine Chandon,
Genentech, Gilead
Sciences, Informix
Corporation, Oracle
Corporation, Sun
Microsystems, Synopsys.

818 Brannan Street
Suite 300
San Francisco, CA 94103
415 621 0915

Cahan & Associates has garnered over 500 awards nationally and internationally throughout the last 10 years. However, Bill Cahan maintains that the real indicator of the firm's success is the 98 percent client return rate. "We're not about fashion or the latest graphic mannerism—we're interested in solving complex problems in an intelligent, accessible manner," says Cahan. Although he often jokes about the statement, "Practice safe design—use a concept," Cahan also feels it is a statement that is central to his firm's philosophy for creating breakthrough design.

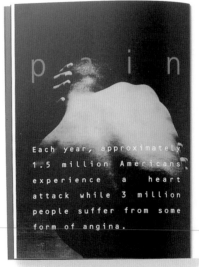

above and right
Annual report for COR Therapeutics, South San Francisco, CA. The company is dedicated to the discovery, development and commercialization of novel pharmaceutical products to treat and prevent cardiovascular diseases. Illustrated by using large single words and photographic images, it depicts the emotion relating to the alarming annual statistics of heart disease, stressing the urgency of the products. Art Director, Bill Cahan; designer, Jean Orlebeke; photography, various.

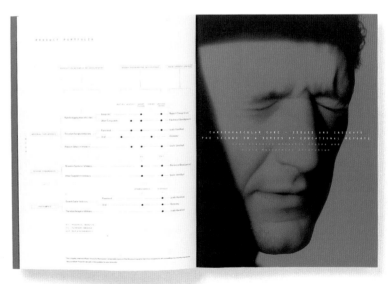

left
Bill Cahan, Principal
and the Cahan &
Associates office.

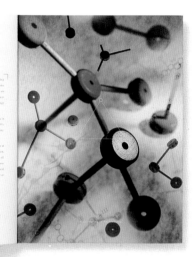

left and above
Annual report for Synopsys,
Inc., Mountain View, CA.
The company provides new
generations of software tools
for electronic design auto-
mation. Imagery of puzzles
represents the problem-solving capabilities of the software. The line diagrams that
appear over each image offer
the solution to the puzzle.
Art Director, Bill Cahan;
designer, Sharrie Brooks;
photography, Kevin Irby.

right
Promotional materials for a
worldwide conference held
by Oracle Corporation,
Redwood Shores, CA. The
label design features a twist-
off cap and a corkscrew as
metaphors for accessibility
of information and the
"user friendly" fashion of the
products. Other materials
include posters, signage, a
multimedia presentation
and various collateral.
Art Director, Bill Cahan;
designer, Bob Dinetz;
photography,
Tony Stromberg.

left
Design for Caffé Roma,
San Francisco, CA. Classic
Italian typography—an
essential feature for this
Italian coffee blend—
placed on a clean, white
background distinguishes
the packaging from its
competitors.
Art Director, Bill Cahan;
designer, Kevin Roberson.

left
Annual report for
Molecular Dynamics,
Sunnyvale, CA. The report
for this developer of life-sci-
ence imaging instruments
needed to be memorable,
but inexpensive. An 11-by-
17-inch format was
designed to fold in half for
storage in an envelope or
file drawer. Instead of photographs or illustrations,
words were used as visuals
to convey the company's
progress for the year.
Art Director, Bill Cahan;
designer, Bob Dinetz.

below
Annual report for Adaptec, Milpitas, CA. The company designs, manufactures and markets a comprehensive family of hardware and software solutions, collectively called IOware products. The comic book style—a powerful, familiar medium to grab the reader's attention—uses colorful, bold visuals to illustrate the company's strategic messages and core competencies.
Art Director, Bill Cahan; designer, Craig Clark; illustrator, Steve Vance.

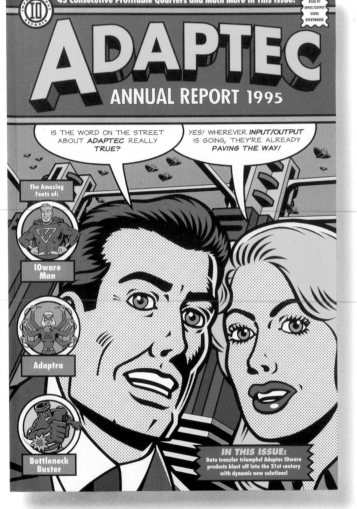

Developing The Future.

Table of Contents.

right
Identity program for
Creative Labs, Milpitas, CA.
As a leader in PC sound,
video and CD-ROM multi-
media solutions, the new
logos developed a strong
identity for the company's
range of products.
Art Director, Bill Cahan;
designer/illustrator,
Sharrie Brooks.

left
Annual report for Informix
Software, Menlo Park, CA.
The company builds data-
base products founded on an
enduring, underlying architecture—a strategy designed
to better enable the customer
with scalable product technology. The company's
strength is communicated
through customer testimoni-
als and stories.
Art Director, Bill Cahan;
designer, Kevin Roberson;
photography, Neal Brown.

Informix

Home Depot

left
Annual report for Oak
Technology, Sunnyvale,
CA. The company enables
interactive multimedia by
developing comprehensive
solutions for PC and con-
sumer electronics manufacturers around the world. To
bring the multimedia experience to the reader, the
report begins with a removable entry ticket, followed
by a series of full-page color
images with key words
describing the action or
emotion connected to the
experience.
Art Director, Bill Cahan;
designer, Craig Clark;
photography, various.

INTERACT
TOUCH

Chip Kidd

Principal: Chip Kidd
Year Founded: 1964
Size of Firm: 1
Key Clients:
Alfred A. Knopf,
Appleton Paper,
Champion Paper,
Cooper-Hewitt Museum,
HarperCollins,
I.D. magazine,
The New Republic,
The New York Times,
Swatch, Virgin Records,
Vogue magazine.

315 East 68th Street
#PH-E
New York, NY 10021
212 879 9503 or
212 572 2363

Chip Kidd is a graphic designer functioning primarily in the world of book design, literature and the arts. His book jacket designs for Alfred A. Knopf have helped spawn a revolution in the art of American book packaging in the last ten years. His work has been featured in *Metropolis, Vanity Fair, The Graphic Edge* (by Rick Poyner), *Eye, Print, Entertainment Weekly, The New Republic, Time, The New York Times, Graphis, New York* and *I.D.* magazines. The latter chose him as part of its first ID 40 group of the nation's top designers. His designs have been described as "Monstrously ugly" (John Updike); "Apparently obvious" (William Boyd); "Faithful flat-earth rendering" (Don DeLillo); "Surprisingly elegant" (A.S. Mehta); "A distinguished parochial comic balding Episcopal priest" (Allan Gurganus); "two colors plus a sash" (Martin Amis); and "Not a piece of hype. My book was lucky." (Robert Hughes).

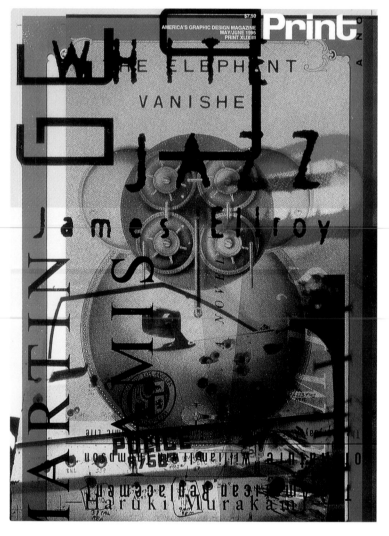

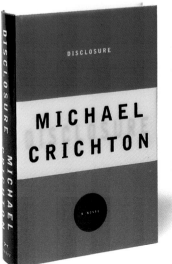

above
Cover for *Print* magazine, New York, NY. The cover accompanied an article by Kidd about designing book jackets and its resulting chaos. The image is made up five different designs layered on top one another. Designer, Chip Kidd.

left
Book jacket for *Disclosure,* Alfred A. Knopf, New York, NY. Designer, Chip Kidd.

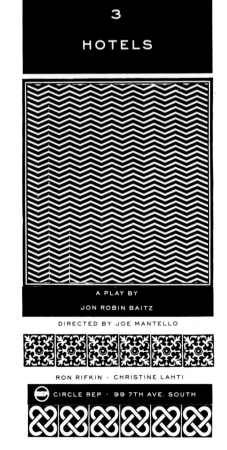

left
Chip Kidd.
Photography,
Marion Ettlinger.

below
Cover and opening spread
of the Kromekote
"Subjective Reasoning"
series for Champion Paper,
Stamford, CT. It concerns
copyright law and Jeff Koon's
appropriation of a photo-
graph, his subsequent sculpture based on it, and the
resulting lawsuit.
Designer, Chip Kidd.

bottom left
Project for *Speak* magazine,
San Fransisco, CA.
Theoretical book jackets:
Mein Kampf by Adolf Hitler,
and *Nine Stories* by
J.D. Salinger.
Art Director, David Carson;
editor, Neil Feineman;
designer, Chip Kidd;
photography, Geoff Spear.

bottom right
Unused newspaper ad and
identity for the play *3 Hotels*
by Jon Robin Baitz, for
Circle Repertory, New
York, NY. The different
patterns represent the
establishments of the title,
which are in three different
foreign countries.
Designer, Chip Kidd.

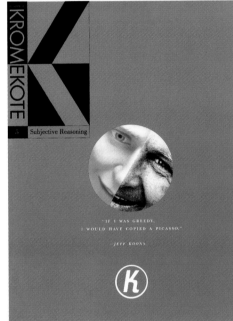

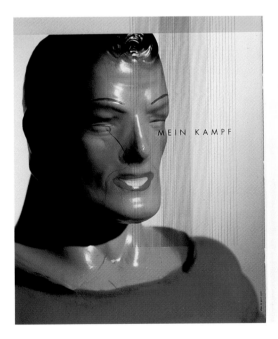

above left
Book jacket and visual
identity for a graphic design
show at the Cooper Hewitt
Museum, New York, NY.
Designer, Chip Kidd.

above center
Book jacket for *American
Illustration*, New York, NY.
Art Director, Chip Kidd;
designer/illustrator,
Chris Ware.

left
Book jacket for *Shiloh*,
HarperCollins,
New York, NY.
Art Director,
Joseph Montebello;
designer, Chip Kidd.

above
Annual report cover for
The Dolder Grand Hotel
in Zürich, Switzerland.
Designer, Chip Kidd.

below
Unused concept for the
Rolling Stone's "Voodoo
Lounge," Virgin Records,
Los Angeles, CA.
Art Director, Len Peltier;
designer, Chip Kidd.

Book jacket and first five spreads of *Chuck Close: Life and Work*, for Anne Yarowsky/Thames & Hudson, New York, NY. This sequence attempts to replicate the experience seeing one of Close's paintings across the room and slowly walking toward it. Designer, Chip Kidd.

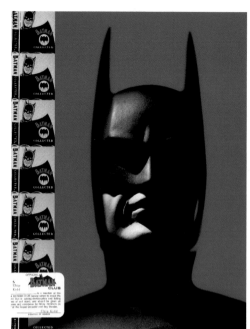

left
Promotional brochure for
Chip Kidd's book, *Batman
Collected*, Bulfinch Press,
Boston, MA. The book por-
trays Batman as an ameri-
can cultural myth.
Designer, Chip Kidd;
photography, Geoff Spear.

below
Illustration for the book
jacket *Jurassic Park*, New
York, NY. This image was
used for the movie's logo
and then appeared throughout the feature film.
Illustrator, Chip Kidd.

right
Cover for *The New
Republic.* Created for an
article about the abuse of
Prozac, Kidd relayed, "I
borrowed the iconography
of cigarette advertisements
that show 'pretty, young
people' enjoying them-
selves, oblivious to any
dangerous behavior that
they might be promoting."
Designer, Chip Kidd.

far right
Cover for *The New
Republic,* Washington, DC.
for an article about the
power of scent.
Designer, Chip Kidd.

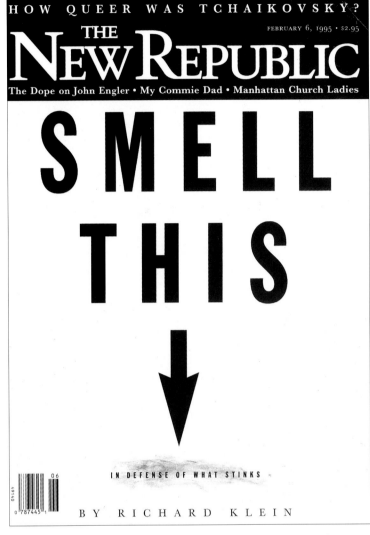

left
Prototype for the redesign
of *The New Republic,*
Washington, DC.
Designer, Chip Kidd.

Cloud and Gehshan Associates, Inc.

Principals: Jerome Cloud, Virginia Gehshan
Year Founded: 1986
Size of Firm: 7
Key Clients: Ayers Saint Gross Architects, Delaware & Lehigh National Heritage Corridor, Downtown Partnership of Baltimore, Ellenzweig Associates, Fairmount Park Commission, Milton Hershey School, New Jersey Transit Light Rail, Orlando Convention Center, Penn's Landing Corporation, Philadelphia Museum of Art, SmithKline Beecham, Singapore Turf Club, Strawberry Square, University of Virginia, Wallace Roberts & Todd.

919 South Street
Philadelphia, PA 19147
215 829 9414

Cloud and Gehshan Associates maintains a diverse practice—blending projects in print, electronic, publication and environmental graphic design. The firm is especially adept at establishing identities for clients that require a variety of applications. Jerome Cloud and Virginia Gehshan believe that design must transcend conventional wisdom and industry formulas to yield solutions with ingenuity and originality. They have practiced this philosophy with innovative projects, both two and three-dimensional. Their designs reflect a unique and personal vision for each client, and manage to find in each problem that which is special and memorable. They strive to express each idea with intelligence and economy; embracing a "less is more" approach by proposing solutions that rely on simplicity, strength and wit rather than gimmicks or excess.

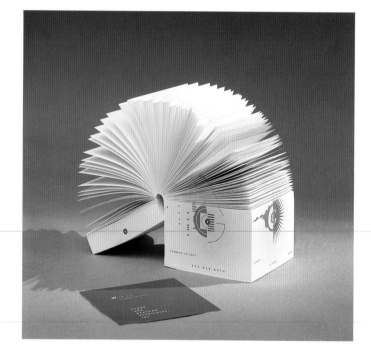

above
Self-promotional note cube. Used as a holiday gift, the cubes came with the greeting, "Wishing you a Happy and Noteworthy New Year." Printed in two color-palettes, four different "CG's" are used to represent expertise in identity, print, signage and communications. Director/Designer, Jerome Cloud.

below right
Logo. Cloud and Gehshan Associates, Inc., Philadelphia, PA. Director, Jerome Cloud; designers, Cloud and Brad Kear.

above and left
Signage for the food court in the Orange County Convention Center, Orlando, FL. The signage utilized oversized cutouts, vivid colors and edge-lit glass. Directors, Virginia Gehshan and Jerome Cloud; designer, Ann McDonald.

left
Virginia Gehshan and
Jerome Cloud.
Photography, Tom Crane.

right
Logo revision for Zany
Brainy, Ardmore, PA. This
energetic logo is highly legible and uses colors that
appear the same in daylight,
as well as when internally
illuminated at night.
Director, Jerome Cloud;
designers, Cloud and
Dorothy Funderwhite.

above
Identity system for
Lamoreaux Landing,
Seneca Lake, NY. Logo,
logotype, neckbands and
bottle designs were created
for a winery on the lake
using distinctive combinations of unusual, pale colors.
Director, Jerome Cloud;
designers, Cloud and
Bradford Kear.

left
Lifetime achievement award
for UniversityCenter in
Baltimore, MD. Made as an
extension to the develop-
ment of its environmental
identity program, the newly
instituted award is a glass
sculpture that uses the same
colors, image and typography.
The double helix image is
sandblasted and the graphics
are silk-screened.
Director, Virginia Gehshan;
designer, Ann McDonald.

below left
Identity for Skylands
Microbrewery, Branchburg,
NJ. The concept reflects
the rural countryside and is
versatile to use in extensive
packaging and promotions.
Director, Virginia Gehshan;
designer, Cheryl Hanba.

left
Poster for Indian Valley
Printing, Souderton, PA.
The marketing poster was
made to celebrate
Indian Valley Printing's
25th anniversary.
Director, Jerome Cloud;
designers, Cloud and
Brad Kear.

right
Logo and identity system for the waterfront ice rink at Penn's Landing, Philadelphia, PA. Creating a unique identity separate from Penn's Landing, applications include signage, banners, uniforms, zamboni machine and rink identification "under ice". The skater with fabric streamers revolves above the main identification sign from the constant river breezes. Directors, Jerome Cloud and Virginia Gehshan; designers, Cloud and Cheryl Hanba (logo); RiverRink name, Cloud.

RiverRink
at Penn's Landing

above and right
This logo uses a whimsical approach for a new downtown bus system with a people-friendly, "low floor," low-polluting vehicle. The dimensional sign is distinctive but still highly vandal and theft resistant. Director, Jerome Cloud; designers, Cloud, Thomas Corlett and Dorothy Funderwhite.

left
Identity for Roach
Wheeler, Devon, PA.
Created for two merging
realty companies, each
with distinct traditions, an
extensive, overnight change-
out of all publications and
signage was accomplished.
Director, Jerome Cloud,
designers, Cloud and
Cheryl Hanba; consultant,
David Boorstin Associates.

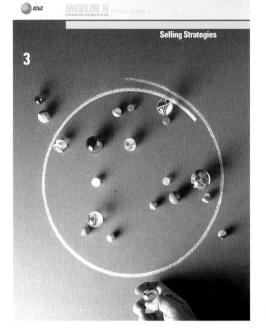

above and opposite page
Series of publications for
AT&T, Princeton, NJ.
Imaginative imagery
instead of product photos is
used to educate the sales
force about the project. A
marble metaphor describes
the process of educating
customers, identifying
markets and closing a sale.
Director, Jerome Cloud;
designers, Ann McDonald
and Cloud.

right
Self-promotional Christmas
card, a creation from the
artist's second grade
poetry class.
Directors, Jerome Cloud
and Virginia Gehshan;
design/copy/illustration,
Julian Cloud; electronic
translation, Thomas Corlett.

above
Sign for the Pennsylvania
Convention Center,
Philadelphia. Light sconces
were designed to high-
light the Overlook Cafe's
balcony location in the
convention center.
Directors, Jerome Cloud
and Virginia Gehshan;
designers, Cloud and
Ann McDonald.

right
Identity for National Park Service, Bethlehem, PA. Created for a five-county region in Pensylvania that was designated a National Heritage Corridor. The challenge was to design a logo to market diverse cultural and natural resources (mountains, rivers, canals and the industrial past). Director/Designer, Jerome Cloud.

below right
Poster for W.L. Gore, Elkton, MD. One from a series of point-of-purchase posters and 14 magazine advertisements in a continuing effort to expand the company's customer base. It promotes the everyday users of Gore-Tex fabric, as well as the sports enthusiast. Director/Designer, Jerome Cloud; photo research, Pamela Pharr.

far right
Sign system for a children's rehabilitation facility, Children's Seashore House, Philadelphia, PA. To improve wayfinding and add personality to the interior spaces, the signs use a "seashore" theme (the original facility was on the Jersey Shore). Tactile/Braille room numbers are integral with the fish shapes. All of the signs' inserts can be generated by the client on laser printers. Director, Jerome Cloud; designers, Cloud and Cheryl Hanba.

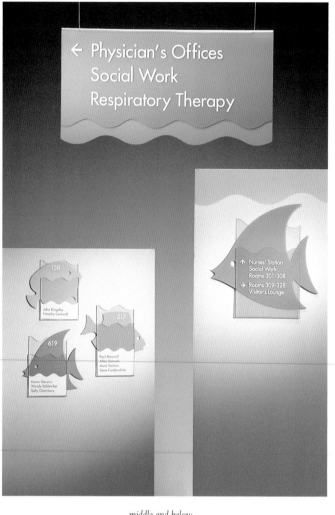

below
Banner for The George Washington University, Washington, DC. Director/Designer, Jerome Cloud.

middle and below
To dramatize the restoration of an elaborate and historic building, banners were made for Philadelphia's City Hall. Director, Virginia Gehshan; designer, Ann McDonald.

Wild Goose House

left
Logo for the Wild Goose House, a historic residence in Chestnut Hill, PA. Director, Jerome Cloud; designers, Cloud and David Schpok.

below left
Identity for Grenald Waldron Associates, architectural lighting consultants, Narberth, PA. Each piece is over-printed with a different color gradation, representing the various color temperatures of light. Directors, Jerome Cloud and Virginia Gehshan; designers, Cloud and Cheryl Hanba.

below right and bottom
Banners for Historic Philadelphia, Inc., PA. To engage the viewer with more than an image, eight different banners were conceived as a series of "broadsides," with stories taken from historic newspapers. The reverse side displays illustrations of the "headlines." 100 banners were hung to announce the historic district. Design Concept, Virginia Gehshan; designer, Jerome Cloud.

below
Banner for UniversityCenter, Baltimore, MD. Director/Writer, Virginia Gehshan; designer, Ann McDonald.

below
Banner program for Penn's Landing Corporation, Philadelphia, PA. Images were designed to reflect three themes: maritime history, entertainment and a working port. All the images, themes and color palettes were extended from the banner to a performing stage, uniforms, trolleys, vendor stands and other decorative enhancements. Directors, Jerome Cloud and Virginia Gehshan; designers, Cloud, Ann McDonald and Bradford Kear.

below
Banner for the Philadelphia Museum of Art, PA. The design had to have an impressionistic flavor without attempting to copy any one painting. Director, Jerome Cloud; designers, Cloud and Thomas Corlett.

below
Banner for the Milton Hershey School, Hershey, PA. Directors, Jerome Cloud and Virginia Gehshan; designer, Cloud.

Cummings & Good

Principals: Peter Good,
Janet Cummings Good
Year Founded: 1971
Size of Firm: 6
Key Clients: Aetna, General
Re Corporation, The
Hartford Steam Boiler
Inspection and Insurance Co.,
Houghton-Mifflin Company,
International Paper,
The Mark Twain House,
Merck & Co., Polaroid
Corporation,
Rossi Enterprises, Special
Olympics World Games,
Strathmore Paper Company,
TheaterWorks.

3 North Main Street
PO Box 570
Chester, CT 06412
203 526 9597

ummings & Good clash, mitigate, question and synthesize. They agree that information is organic, everyone communicates, but not everyone knows how or what. Janet Cummings and Peter Good share the tenacity to have survived (mostly gracefully) three decades of collaborating in art, marriage, parenting and business. They have learned to constantly adapt to life's vagaries, sometimes in dramatic ways. In 1995 they completely restructured their studio, hired four exceptional people with diverse skills but similar work ethics, and changed the business name to credit Janet's full-time commitment. The Cummings & Good approach to design reflects the experience of the couple's lives; sagacious and self-confident, it also can be spontaneous and whimsical. Embracing technology, they have retained the principles of form based on imaginative and intelligent content, a Hegelian approach to typography and excruciating attention to detail. In the center of a vibrant Connecticut river-valley town, the internationally known studio occupies the sun-drenched top floor in a landmark Greek Revival building—with a back deck for barbecues and office cat, Emma. Cummings & Good believe that design is not as important as life, but more of life can be brought to design.

left
Left to right:
Michell A. Parr Paulson,
Christine Turner,
Christopher J Hyde,
Deborah E. Walls,
Peter Good,
Janet Cummings Good
Photography, Richard Frank.

opposite page left
Series of holiday stamps for
the U.S. Postal Service,
Washington, D.C. The
stamps were created to be
adaptable to a variety of
stamp formats; sheets,
booklets, ATM coils and
pressure sensitive. The
Love Stamp empowers a
small space with a visual
expression—love as a
metaphorical sunrise.
Designer/Illustrator,
Peter Good.

below
Identity system for the
Special Olympics World
Games Organizing
Committee, New Haven,
CT. The system needed to
coordinate a world games
logo with sports and special
events venues. It uses an
element from the master
logo, connecting the games
logo with different venues
and symbols. The symbols
were reproduced on mil-
lions of products, sportswear,
banners, signs and elec-
tronic transmissions.
Designer, Peter Good;
production, Ed Kim and
Deborah Walls.

left
Poster for the Hospital for
Special Care, New Britain,
CT. The image—meta-
phorically referenced to
rehabilitation—is sewn fab-
ric, created to use for a
commemorative poster and
further applications.
Designer/Illustrator,
Peter Good; concept,
Janet Cummings Good.

above
Swatchbook for Arjo-
Wiggins USA, Greenwich,
CT. Designed as a pun on
printers' plates, the reverse
side of the swatchbook
reflects the reverse aspects
of printers film, and unex-
pectedly the underside of
the plate.
Designer, Christopher Hyde.

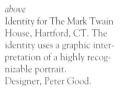

left
Visual identity for Chatham
Printing, Newington, CT.
The logo combines the let-
terform "C" with a pulsating
dot matrix, eluding to energy,
electronics and printing.
Designers, Peter Good and
Christopher Hyde.

above
Identity for The Mark Twain
House, Hartford, CT. The
identity uses a graphic interpretation of a highly recognizable portrait.
Designer, Peter Good.

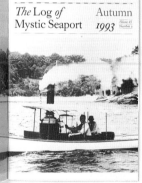

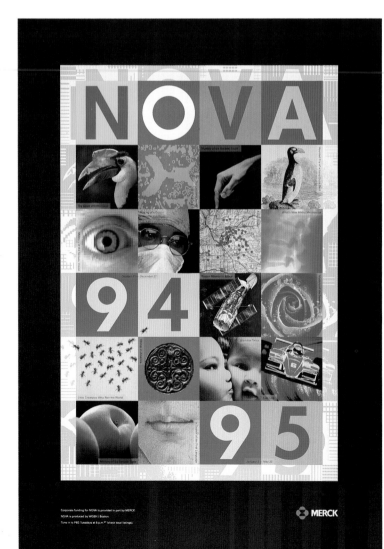

left
Poster for Merck & Co.,
Whitehouse Station, NJ.
The poster expresses the
dramatic programming of
the public television science
series, *Nova*.
Designers, Peter Good and
Janet Cummings Good;
illustrator, Janet Cummings
Good; photography, various.

above
Quarterly publication for
members of the Mystic
Seaport Museum, Mystic,
CT. The publication relates
a one-color mailer flap pro-
tector with a two-color cover.
Designers, Peter Good,
Ed Kim.

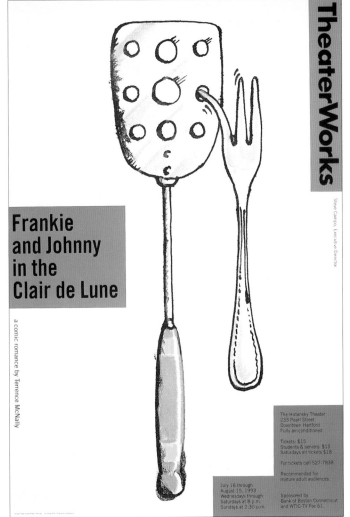

top left
Poster for TheaterWorks, Hartford, CT. To announce the play "Scotland Road," the poster used a vernacular tabloid form to express the play, which was inspired by the tabloid.
Designer/Fabricator, Peter Good; photography, Jim Coon.

left
Poster for TheaterWorks. A romance between a short order cook and a waitress is expressed using "consenting" utensils.
Designer/Illustrator, Peter Good.

above
Poster for Rossi Enterprises, Haddam, CT. To create the awareness of Rossi Lumber as a source of American Hardwoods for export, the poster's concept uses a quintessential American object to show the seven species of wood.
Designers, Peter Good, Janet Cummings Good and Christopher Hyde; photography, Sean Kernan.

above and right
Identity, brochure and poster for the Connecticut Impressionist Art Trail, Old Lyme. The identity informs and creates an awareness about a tour of Connecticut museums that have a connection to American Impressionism. The poster (*far right*) uses art materials to suggest the period. The paint tubes identify the participating museums. Designers, Peter Good and Christopher Hyde; photography, Sean Kernan (poster) and Jim Coon (brochure).

below left
One of an ad series on environmental endeavors for International Paper, Purchase, NY. The ads tell factual stories about the company's experts working on environmental projects. Designer, Peter Good; photography, Jack McConnell.

below
The note cards demonstrate International Paper's flowers, waters, forests and fields. Package designer, Christopher Hyde.

opposite page right
Cover designs for Houghton-Mifflin, Boston, MA. *Wildflowers* is part of a series using classic typography and illustration for traditional subject matter. Designer, Peter Good; designer/illustrator, Janet Cummings Good. The *Cultural Dictionary* has a simple, appealing cover. Fabric textures are used to express a variety of different cultures. Designer, Peter Good.

Dr. "Si" Jahromi: Family Man

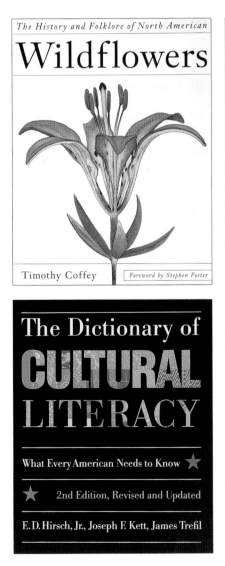

The History and Folklore of North American

Wildflowers

Timothy Coffey   *Foreword by Stephen Foster*

The Dictionary of
CULTURAL
LITERACY

What Every American Needs to Know ★

★ 2nd Edition, Revised and Updated

E. D. Hirsch, Jr., Joseph F. Kett, James Trefil

Stamped, sealed and delivered.
Aetna Health Plans commissions a series of stamps,
introduces a new look for 1995.

 Aetna
Health
Plans

above
Poster for Unisource,
Windsor, CT. To create a
poster as a complement to
a calendar using the same
image, the position of the
letterform "C" was changed,
and the meaning of "change"
is expressed as "chance."
The "chance" connection
with "change" occurred
during the process of design.
Designers, Peter Good and
Janet Cummings Good;
construction, Peter Good;
concept, Janet Cummings
Good; photography,
Jim Coon.

left
Campaign materials and
guidelines for Aetna Health
Plans, Middletown, CT.
The system emphasizes
choice through a collection
of stamp-like icons that
change according to the
requirements of each health
plan, helping to unify and
humanize numerous pieces
of a complex health care
system.
Designers/Illustrators,
Peter Good and
Janet Cummings Good.

DESIGN!

Principals: Bill Grant,
Russ Ramage
Year Founded: 1989
Size of Firm: 7
Key Clients: Creative Arts
Guild, Dalton Little
Theatre, Interface, Inc.,
Interface Europe, Ltd.,
Interface Flooring Systems,
Lotus Carpets, Prince Street
Technologies, Ltd.,
The Peregrinzilla Press.

809 Chattanooga Avenue
Dalton, Georgia 30720
706 272 3770

i.e., design
111 East Marietta Street
Suite 300
P.O. Box 1910
Canton, Georgia 30114
770 479 8280

ESIGN! was founded by principals Bill Grant and Russ Ramage who view great design as great thinking. The partners believe intelligent design communicates clearly, solves problems, evokes emotions, provides inspiration and creates real-world opportunities. The origin of design creates a dichotomy: design has value, sells products and services, and yet must meet these criteria with simple elegance. With a penchant for classic design executed with this simplicity, DESIGN! has been recognized for solving complicated communication problems with smart design solutions. With a passionate commitment to maintaining the quality of their work, the principals embarked on separate journeys in 1996. Ramage accepted an in-house design position with Interface Americas. Grant formed i.e., design with a diversified staff and client base.

left
Clothbound book with dust jacket of *Eitel Time*, for The Peregrinzilla Press, Atlanta, GA. The 96-page book illustrates the author's personal management style, which is based on his symbolic "clock of accountability."
Designers, DESIGN!;
author, Charlie Eitel;
photography, Jerry Burns;
printer, The Stinehour Press.

above
Poster/mailer outlining the components of the Industry & Ecology program for Collins & Aikman, Dalton, GA. The poster was used as both a promotional piece and invitation. It was folded and imprinted with information on several industry trade shows.
Designers, DESIGN!;
photography, Jerry Burns.

left
From left: Bill Grant, Reva Poston, Cheryl Creswell, Vicki Strull, Judy Reed and Russ Ramage.
Photography, Jerry Burns.

right
Logomark for Bill Grant's new firm, i.e., design.

i.e.

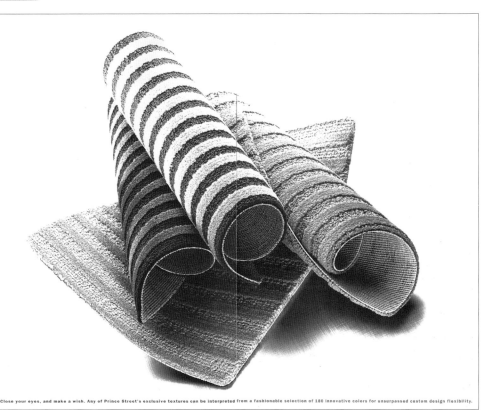

Close your eyes, and make a wish. Any of Prince Street's exclusive textures can be interpreted from a fashionable selection of 180 innovative colors for unsurpassed custom design flexibility.

We're not getting older; we're getting better. Prince Street assures quality and performance with proprietary manufacturing techniques, type 6,6 nylon and full-circle technical assistance.

PRIN CE ST REET

A 12-page, two-color tabloid for Prince Street Technologies Ltd., Cartersville, GA. The company produces high-fashion commercial carpets. The tabloid celebrates the company's 10th birthday and addresses the facets of its business that have made it successful in its field. The tabloid worked to position the product as fashion, as well as serving as a corporate capabilities brochure, a pull-through for its advertising campaign and a birthday celebration piece. Designers, DESIGN!; "Prince" photography, Jerry Burns; product photography, Greg Slater.

below left
Company-overview brochure for Interface Flooring Systems, LaGrange, GA. As the world's largest producer of commercial carpet tiles, the 24-page brochure outlined the new management's re-engineering process and was an integral component in the introduction of a new brand identity and image for the company. It addressed its heritage and future, product design, manufacturing technology and cultural revolution.

Designers, DESIGN!; illustration photography, Geof Kern; architectural photography, William Abranowicz

below right
Two of four 1994 trade advertisements for Interface Flooring Systems. "Direction" and "Left.Right." spreads appeared in commercial design trade publications such as *Interior Design* and *Metropolis* magazines. The campaign was designed to reintroduce the company's brand to architects and interior designers; detailing the heritage, future and "direction" of the company. Designers, DESIGN!; photography, Geof Kern.

right
Self-promotional logo. Designers, DESIGN!

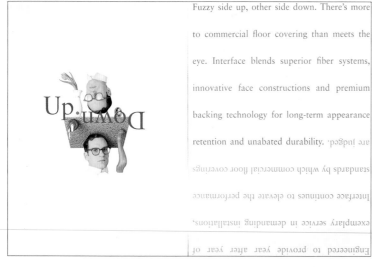

Fuzzy side up, other side down. There's more to commercial floor covering than meets the eye. Interface blends superior fiber systems, innovative face constructions and premium backing technology for long-term appearance retention and unabated durability. are judged.

standards by which commercial floor coverings

Interface continues to elevate the performance

exemplary service in demanding installations,

Engineered to provide year after year of

Direction. Interface Flooring Systems is on the move. The world's leading commercial carpet manufacturer is charting a new course of action in response to the evolving needs of global customers. From carpet tiles to six foot roll goods, our products will remain benchmarks in styling and performance. When it comes to superior commercial floor covering, let Interface be your guide. Interface.

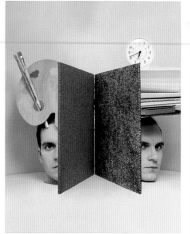

Left. Right. Left-Brainers adhere to reason and practicality. Right-Brainers have a more creative outlook. Interface knows it takes both to produce stylish commercial carpets with unprecedented performance features. When it comes to superior commercial carpet, look both ways to Interface.

left
Cardboard shopping bag and lunch box for Interface Flooring Systems. The shopping "bax," a term coined by DESIGN!, was created to hold several 18-inch by 18-inch carpet tiles and distributed at trade shows and design-center showrooms. The bag also became a walking billboard for the new logo and identity. The lunch box, is a multi-purpose container. "Since food is the quickest way to anyone's mind, the lunch box became another great vehicle to display and introduce the new image program for Interface." Designers, DESIGN!

below left
Sample binder for Interface Flooring Systems. The eco-friendly industry sample binder replaces the normally excessive ones. It is made of chipboard with an debossed logo; the spine has a bio-degradable reinforcement, the plastic trays were replaced with a constructed layer of corrugated cardboard and a layer of chipboard laminated with recycled paper. The binder can be placed in a shredder to create recycled chipboard.
Designers, DESIGN!

bottom left
"Restore" and "Renew," two of three advertisements created for Interface Flooring Systems' 1995 trade advertising campaign. The Editorial informs the reader about environmental issues related to the field.
Designers, DESIGN!; photography, Geof Kern.

right
Wordmark and logo for Interface Flooring System's Why? Conference. Offered to interior designers and architects, the conference's program was about personal development or "outward bound." The logo appeared on invitations, T-shirts, caps, and other paraphernalia.
Designers, DESIGN!

Renew. What goes around comes around. Interface Flooring Systems believes waste equals food in a fragile material economy. In an attempt to mimic nature's own restorative process, the company is turning used commercial floorcovering into new products or energy. Basically, everything old is new again. If you are practicing sustainable design, one company has a growing interest in being your partner: Interface.

Restore. What goes down must come up. Natural law now prohibits the replacement and disposal of entire floors. As pioneers of modular carpeting technology, Interface Flooring Systems explores a few alternatives: selective replacement in high traffic areas, interchangeable pattern by tile or even floorcovering leases. If you're following the path to sustainable design, one company is laying the groundwork: Interface.

above and right
"Re:" merchandising elements for Interface Flooring Systems. The "bax" was updated and other promotional materials, such as a corresponding brochure, memo pads and pencils, were created to educate customers about what had transpired over the last year with the company. The "Re" prefix also correlates with the ad campaign focused on its "reduce, restore, renew" program.
Designers, DESIGN!

left
Logo created to promote the community Outreach programs by St. Marks Episcopal Church, Dalton, GA. Designers, DESIGN!

below
Trade advertising campaign for Lotus Carpets, Phoenix City, AL. The campaign worked to increase brand recognition among interior designers and architects. It was such a success that a commemorative poster was made from the series, which featured a total of six ads. The company has since doubled its business in one year. Designers, DESIGN!; photography, Geof Kern.

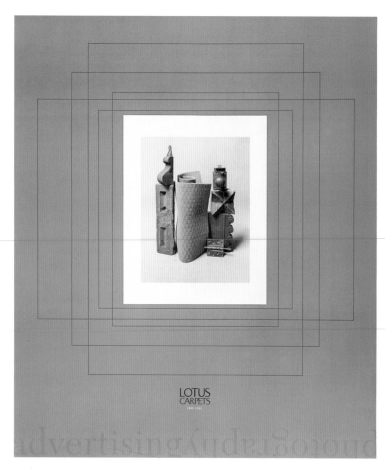

right
The 20-page brochure promotes the products and services offered by Lotus. Designers, DESIGN!; photography, Jerry Burns.

below
Capabilities brochure for
Collins & Aikman, Dalton,
GA. The 18-page brochure
was used to commemorate
the company's 25th ann-
iversary. A "Silver to Gold"
theme was created while
defining the core compo-
nents of the company. The
periodic table symbols were
used as silver and gold, and
gave the brochure the
"Elements" theme.
Designers, DESIGN!;
photography, Maria Robledo.

right and bottom right
Posters for the Creative Arts
Guild and BASF Fibers,
Dalton, GA. Sent to both
art schools and artists, the
posters served as a call for
entries to an annual international design competition
for fiber artists.
Designers, DESIGN!;
photography, Jerry Burns.

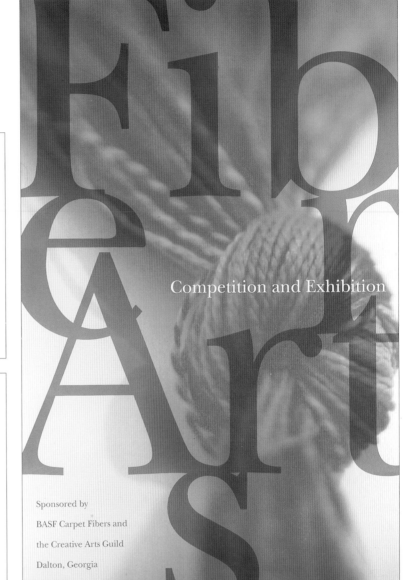

Competition and Exhibition

Sponsored by

BASF Carpet Fibers and

the Creative Arts Guild

Dalton, Georgia

5 October - 1 November 1993

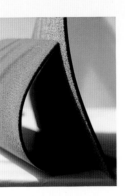

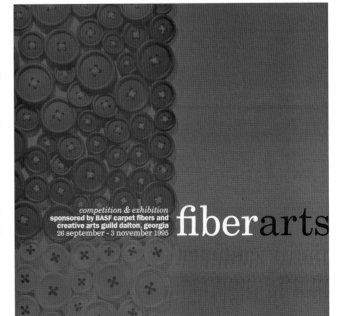

competition & exhibition
sponsored by BASF carpet fibers and
creative arts guild dalton, georgia
26 september - 3 november 1995   **fiber**arts

Ema Design Inc.

Principal: Thomas Courtenay Ema
Year Founded: 1982
Size of Firm: 3
Key Clients: ACX Technologies Incorporated, Artist's Angle Incorporated, BI Incorporated, Canyon Resources, CIBER, Incorporated; CyberCon Construction Corporation, Interenergy Corporation, MCC Construction Corporation, Neenah Paper Company, Nouveau Properties, LLC; Plains Petroleum Company, Tremont Corporation.

1228 15th Street
Suite 301
Denver, CO 80202
303 825 0222

e ma Design focuses on making ideas accessible through design. Principal Thomas Courtenay Ema and his staff begin their process by clarifying each client's communication objectives. "Once we identify and prioritize the benefits of their products or services, we look for connections that exist between those benefits and the world around us," says Ema. "We find metaphorical parallels or associations that become the seeds of our design approach. From there, we fill the functional need with a creative solution that is rooted in clear logic, but expressed through beauty." Ema believes that even the most solid and practical solution is best expressed with grace, rhythm and balance. "Many people have told us that our work more than looks good—it makes them feel good," he says. "Maybe bringing a little beauty and warmth into the world is not a bad contribution to make today."

above
Series of holiday theme postcards for Artist's Angle Inc., Denver, CO, a graphic arts support service. The postcards serve as a reminder to use the services described on the back of the cards. Designers, Thomas C. Ema and Debra Johnson Humphrey; illustrator, Ema.

left
Logo for Artist's Angle Inc. In order to create an identity that connects with the artist in each client, the letterforms were hand drawn and painted. Designer, Thomas C. Ema.

left
Thomas Courtenay Ema.
Photography,
Stephen Ramsey.

below
Letterhead box for Neenah
Paper, Atlanta, GA. The
Kimberly Writing Letterhead
Box contains samples of
letterhead paper, printed
samples of paper and a swatchbook with the paper held
in place by a die-cut insert.
The upscale redesign presents
the product in a coordinated
and distinctive manner.
Designers, Thomas C. Ema
and Debra Johnson
Humphrey.

right
Poster/mailer for AIGA,
Denver, CO, promoting a
lecture by Michael Bierut
of Pentagram. Visual
tension is created by using
an extreme close-up of
Bierut. Meaning is added
through Bierut's confessional
quote, "I like to watch."
Designers, Thomas C. Ema,
Debra Johnson Humphrey
and Robin H. Ridley.

Magazine ads for MCC Construction Corporation. The conceptual approach of the series communicates the ideas of cost, time and management. Designers, Thomas C. Ema and Debra Johnson Humphrey; photography, Allen Kennedy.

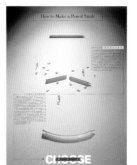

Corporate brochure for MCC Construction Corporation. The concept is to visit various markets with which the company either works or would like to work, such as colleges, manufacturing locations and hospitals. The customer is showcased first in color. The market or location is showcased second, in black and white; and the company is third, represented in small detail shots. Designers, Thomas C. Ema and Debra Johnson Humphrey; photography, Joel Grimes Photography.

PLAINS
PETROLEUM
COMPANY

below
Annual reports for ACX Technologies, BI Incorporated, Tremont Corporation, Canyon Resources, Plains Petroleum Company and CIBER, Incorporated. The intent is to communicate to the reader the unique qualities about each of these companies within the diverse fields of mining, energy, technology, computers and corrections.
Designers, Thomas C. Ema, Debra Johnson Humphrey and Robin H. Ridley.

right
Logo for Plains Petroleum Company, Denver, CO, a natural gas energy company with principal properties in southwest Kansas. Utilizing cut and torn paper, the logo contains the silhouette of a pump jack, symbolizing a producing well in the context of a landscape reminiscent of Kansas farmland. Designer, Thomas C. Ema.

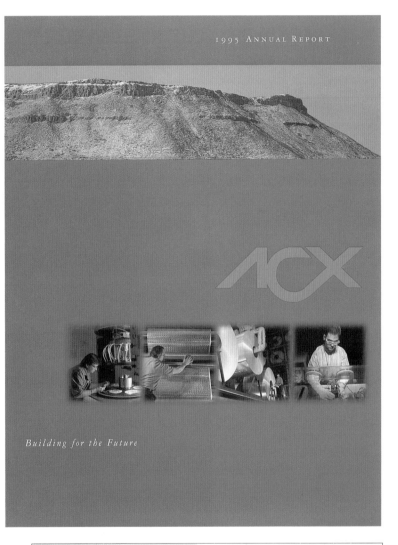

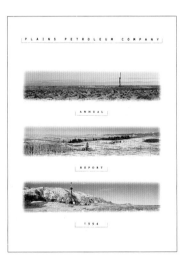

CENTURY LOFTS

right

Name and logo for a thirty-unit downtown Denver loft development project, Nouveau Properties, LLC; Denver, CO. The unusual palette suggests colors used in the Art-Deco buildings in the South Beach area of Miami, Florida.
Designers, Thomas C. Ema, Debra Johnson Humphrey and Robin H. Ridley.

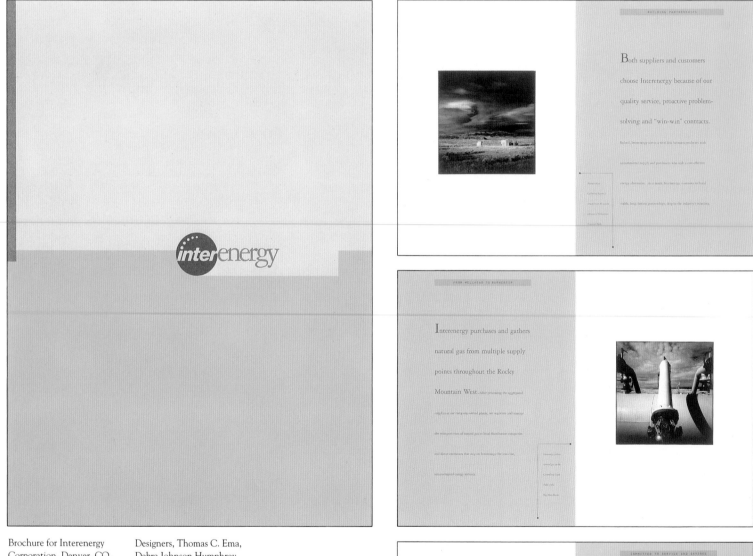

Brochure for Interenergy Corporation, Denver, CO. Beautiful, interesting photos of the company's facilities in northern Wyoming and large, easy to read type at the beginning of sentences help to pull readers into the piece. The pipe photo on the second spread takes on the appearance of a face. A 20-page, self-cover brochure was utilized out of just two forms of 65-pound cover stock (one dull coated and one gray text). Printing was limited to four colors per form to maintain an efficient, effective brochure.

Designers, Thomas C. Ema, Debra Johnson Humphrey and Robin H. Ridley; photography, Stephen Ramsey; copywriter, Sylvia Angell.

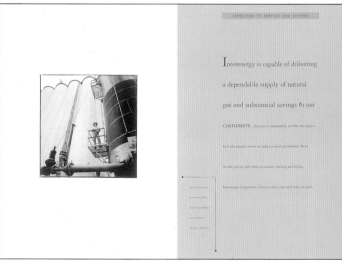

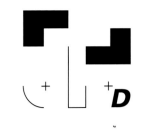

below
Brochure for CyberCon Corporation, Denver, CO. The company's capabilities and process are compared to similar things in nature (Unique structures=nautilus shell, strategic partnerships=ant carrying leaf, harmonious environments=red rock cavern).
Designers, Thomas C. Ema and Debra Johnson Humphrey; corporate photography, Todd Droy.

right
Logo for Todd Droy Photography, Denver, CO. In order to capture the interest of the design community, as well as to communicate some of the characteristics of the photographer's name, the letterforms "T" and "D" were created to fit his precise style and manner of working. Designer, Thomas C. Ema.

Firehouse 101
Art + Design

Principal: Kirk Richard Smith
Year Founded: 1990
Size of Firm: 2
Key Clients: Arista Records, CompuServe, Doubleday, Levi Strauss & Co., Limited Too, Nickelodeon, Ohio Arts Council, Structure, Simon & Schuster, Sony Music, Virgin Interactive Entertainment, Word Records.

492 Armstrong Street
Columbus, OH 43215
614 464 0928

irehouse 101 Art + Design creates graphic design and illustration that challenges traditional definitions— attempting to become more intuitive as art in its communication. The studio goes beyond basic problem solving to introduce elements of emotion, spontaneity and passion within the communication process. "I think our work is most effective when it evokes a disturbing beauty," says Kirk Richard Smith. "By disturbing, I mean the quality to peel back an additional layer of obviousness to invite human emotions into the communication process." Firehouse 101 specializes in full service design and illustration, including logo and identity systems, CD packaging, brochures, posters, animation, book covers and fashion wear.

right
Catalog showcasing artwork for Spaces Gallery, Cleveland, OH. The curators of the gallery created an exhibition that was an artistic exploration in response to HIV/ AIDS, and became an informative vehicle to the public. A single red X on the catalog's cover conveyed the immediacy of the subject and later carried over to the gallery's windows to achieve the same effect.
Art Directors, Kirk Richard Smith and Micheal Milligan; designers, Smith and Terry Alan Rohrbach; illustrator, Smith; photography, Will Shively; copy, Milligan and Susan P. Channing; Jeffrey D. Grove and Wendell Ricketts, (curators of Spaces Gallery).

above
Self promotional tool of a combined poster-turned-brochure format. Sent to record companies and book publishers, the piece was a collaborative effort, co-sponsored by printing and paper companies. It communicated an attitude of emotion in graphic design. Art Director/ Designer/ Illustrator, Kirk Richard Smith; creative contributor, Charles Wagner; photography, Will Shively.

left
Kirk Richard Smith.
Photography, Will Shively
(Shively Photography).

Logo for Lee Hunt Associates/
Intro Television, New York,
NY. The design is immediate
and easy to read, supporting
a recognizable eye as a visual
double-meaning.
Marketing Director, Lee Hunt
(Lee Hunt Associates);
creative director, Cheri Dorr
(Melon Design Worldwide);
designer/illustrator, Kirk
Richard Smith; design assistant, Terry Alan Rohrbach.

Logo for the American
Heart Association,
Columbus, OH. Hand drawn
with india ink and brush,
the logo was created for a
benefit dinner party serving
Carribean food. It was kept
loose in attitude to reflect
the Carribean personality.
Marketing Director,
Tuesday Trippier;
designer/illustrator,
Kirk Richard Smith.

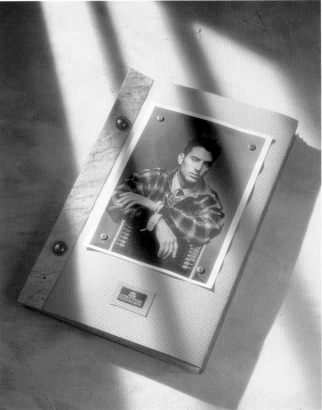

right
The logo conveys a classic
Italian heritage for the
men's retail clothing store,
Structure, Columbus, OH.
The lion illustration, taken
from a Lira note and the
spoked wheel border gives
a strong, architecturally-
graphic feeling.

above and top left
Employee booklet that
educates the internal marketing staff about Structure's
founder, Stephano Villarini.
Used as a reminder of the
personality created for
Structure's identity, all of
the papers, calligraphy and
found artifacts were authen-
tic to the many subject
matters shared about the
history of Italy and Villarini.

Creative Director, David
Brown (Structure);
art director/designer,
Kirk Richard Smith; design
assistants, Terry Alan
Rohrbach (book), and
Charles Wagner (logo);
calligraphy, Smith; photo
transfers; Will Shively.

left
Poster for The Columbus Society of Communicating Arts, OH, a non-profit organization that caters to the professional graphic design, photography, illustration and copywriting audiences. The society wanted to utilize the community in the creative process. The poster was a call for submission—the general public called to submit their dreams on an answering machine. The result of the phone calls later became the copy and visual stimulation that made the photographic collage. Designer/Calligraphy, Kirk Richard Smith; photography, Steven Webster; creative contributor, Charles Wagner.

left
CD cover for the band The Bogmen, Arista Records, New York, NY. Painted on wood with collaged labels from bug spray manufacturers and 1950's girl magazines, the elements chosen related to the attitude and lyrics of the songs. Art Director, Sherri Whitmarsh; illustrator, Kirk Richard Smith.

below
Self-promotional poster. Brought together by donations, the poster itself was designed as a vignette that explored emotional attitude in design. The target audiences were record companies, book publishers and the entertainment community. Art Director/Designer/Illustrator/Calligraphy, Kirk Richard Smith; photography, Will Shively.

below left
Merchandising standards notebook for Levi Strauss & Co., San Francisco, CA. The notebook categorized each type of store display unit and showed the variations of displaying the product in a manner that was easy enough for 500 different store managers to assemble in their own stores. It also made all of the Original Levi's Stores to be consistent in its presentation while allowing flexibility for the individual managers to choose what works best for each store. Focusing on the history of the company—archival images were used of the original building, miners, cowboys, the original logo and the signature of Levi Strauss—as graphic section dividers.
Art Director, Kirk Richard Smith; designers, Smith and Charles Wagner; director of visual merchandising, Tim Sullivan (Levi Strauss & Co.); digital illustrations, Debra Norbie (Levi Strauss & Co.).

below right
Book cover for Doubleday, New York, NY. To illustrate the topic of shame in relation to the gay/lesbian experience, the book exposes the role of shame and the power it has to shape an individual's development of self-esteem, identity and intimacy within the gay/lesbian lifestyles.
Art Directors, Russell Gordon and Kirk Richard Smith; designer, Smith and Terry Alan Rohrbach; photography, Photonica.

right
CD cover for College Music Journal, Great Neck, NY. The painting involved an eclectic approach of combining found wood, a 1940's yam label and acrylic paint to achieve an alternative feel to the final cover. A musical demon was used to conjure up the announcement of certain damage. It was an appropriate figure for the audience—college alternative listeners, DJ's, producers and record labels.
Art Director, Alley Rutzell (CMJ); illustrator, Kirk Richard Smith.

left
Animation spots for Nickelodeon, New York, NY. Nickelodeon created a different "Nick Day" for every day of the year. All the animation art was produced by hand utilizing acrylic paint and ink on cigar box wood, paper and acetate.
Art Directors, Marianna Gracey (Corey McPherson Nash) and Kirk Richard Smith; illustrator, Smith.

right
Illustration for Ray Gun Magazine, San Diego, CA. The illustration, published in the Sound In Print department of the magazine, interprets Morrissey's song, *I've Changed My Plea to Guilty.* "One of the biggest challenges in illustration or design is to be able to produce to your own visual standards. Especially when no boundaries are given," said Smith. "I tried to use symbolic elements of happiness, entrapment and a more obvious imprisonment to relate to the song's theme of confessional love and guilt."
Art Director, David Carson (Ray Gun Magazine); illustrator, Kirk Richard Smith.

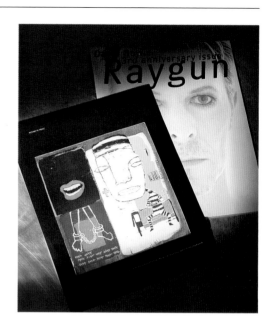

left
Poster for the Semple-Upham Culture + Arts Center, Mount Vernon, OH. The poster announces a show of drawings, paintings, sculptures and animation by Ohio folk artists, David and Amy Butler. It highlights each artist independently, but also shows the common ground in their combined philosophy towards creating art.
Art Director/Designer, Kirk Richard Smith; photography, Will Shively, sculptures, David and Amy Butler (Art of the Midwest).

left
Locomotion channel presentation box for Highgate Properties, New York, NY. Created for a 24 hour cartoon channel in Latin America, the box is used as an announcement to clients. Each side of the 18-inch square box focuses on different marketing aspects and purposes of the logo identity.
Marketing Director, Monica Halpert (Highgate Properties); art directors, Kirk Richard Smith and Holly Chasin (Holly Chasin Design); designers, Smith and Keith Novicki; digital illustrators, Novicki and Marcelle Knittel; painting/hand calligraphy, Smith; additional creative participants, Brad Egnor.

below
Locomotion channel logo. The logo utilizes the typography as facial elements in addition to creating the name. The symbol was created by hand to keep a more spontaneous, human feel.
Marketing Director, Monica Halpert (Highgate Properties); art directors, Kirk Richard Smith and Holly Chasin (Holly Chasin Design); designer/ illustrator, Smith.

far left
International Annual of Design cover for HOW Magazine, Cincinnati, OH. The wood that the image was painted on came from a shelf from Kirk Richard Smith's laundry room. "I think that this is unique only in the fact that as artist we half pull our inspiration and often our materials from whatever is close to our environment," said Smith. "The general idea revolved around this wing messenger of design awaiting the birth of new directions." Other collage materials included labels from the 1940s, world atlas pages and acrylic paint. The illustration was produced in hopes that it would represent the spirit of design in an abstract/ metaphorical way.
Art Director, Scott Fink (HOW Magazine); illustrator, Kirk Richard Smith.

right
Cover of the Christmas of Hope CD, for Sony Music, New York, NY. The album cover was painted on wood and collaged with miscellaneous labels from the 1940's and 1950's. The Christmas feel was maintained without getting too obvious with "color stereotypes."
Art Director, Sean Evans; illustrator,
Kirk Richard Smith.

Gary Koepke

Agency:
Wieden & Kennedy

320 SW Washington
Portland, OR 97204
503 228 4381

Gary Koepke made a monumental step by joining an advertising agency Weiden & Kennedy in May 1996. As principal of Koepke International, Ltd.; established in 1986, he offered custom publication and design, and helped to create *World Tour*, *Soho Journal* and *Vibe*. In addition, Koepke has worked with clients ranging from David Byrne to Benneton. "While noted for his risk-taking tactics, Koepke is in fact something of a classicist in disguise, one who's quick to argue for a simple truth, like the importance of good writing to publication," wrote Steven Heller in *Print*. Consistently reinventing his own style, Kopeke's work is a stead fast process. "If you start defining yourself in terms of what someone else has done" Koepke says, "then it's unlikely you'll end up with anything new."

O nobly born

the time hath now come for thee to seek the Path

thy breathing is about to cease

you are face to face before the Clear Light

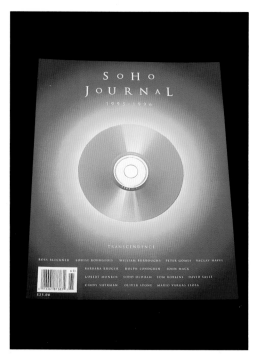

The pain and hunger penetrates my body. The hungry ghosts I see are real people. Through all its existence the body is a house aflame

FEAR + DESIRE   RED ALER
RED ALERT FEAR + DESIR

left
Gary Koepke pictured
in the foreground.
Photography,
John Goodman.

SoHo Journal, New York, NY.
The annual publication,
published by the non-
profit organization SoHo
Partnership, helps to create
neighborhood employment
for the area's homeless.

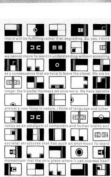

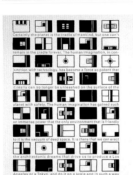

Vibe Magazine, a monthly
music and entertainment
magazine. Founded by
Quincy Jones and published
by Time Ventures, Inc.,
New York, NY.

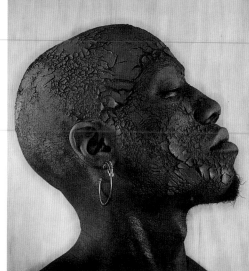

VIBE

GEORGE CLINTON

The Vibe Q by Vernon Reid

Chaka Khan:
Every Woman
(and then some)

THE FUNK HALL OF FAME PLUS: **A TRIBE CALLED QUEST • BOYZ II MEN**
APACHE INDIAN • JOHN LEGUIZAMO • ZHANÉ • RIDDICK BOWE • HEAVY D'S BEDROOM

The Vibe Q

THE TROUBLE WITH WESLEY

*Wesley Snipes crashes motorcycles, packs a semiautomatic,
and beats up the bad guys. Onscreen and off. Danyel Smith catches the first black action
hero on his day off from living the life of a Hollywood bad boy.*

Photographs by Dan Winters

BRIGHT LIGHTS, BIG CITY
Suit by Jiyio Johnson.

the real world

THE MAN WHO FELL TO EARTH
White cotton button-down shirt by Brooks Brothers; pants by Levi's

Grin and Bare It

A MONG HER

AFTER ALL THE CLOWNS
HAVE GONE TO BED

On the beaches of Negril, Jamaica, anything can be had for a price. Except, of course, love. By Joan Morgan

Photographs by Christian Witkin

PIMPER'S PARADISE

VIBe
BOW WOW WOW

Snoop Doggy Dogg
has his day
by Kevin Powell

THE REBIRTH OF COOL STYLE
THE VIBE Q: CORNEL WEST SWV NAILS IT WHAT MAKES PUFFY RUN?

BETTER DAYS

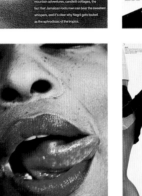

aaron HALL

mc LYTE

World Tour, a quarterly magazine/information digest offered to upper management executives. Published by Dun & Bradstreet Software, New York, NY.

A mind that is stretched to a new idea never returns to its original dimension

Oliver Wendell Holmes

Right: Isamu Noguchi, One Thousand Horsepower Heart.

WoRld ToUR

A REVIEW OF WORLDWIDE BUSINESS AND TECHNOLOGY NEWS PUBLISHED BY DUN & BRADSTREET SOFTWARE   VOLUME 3 NO. 1 JANUARY–MARCH 1993

THERE IS AN EXTORTION OF THE WILL BEYOND ANY OF OUR MEASURE IN THE EXHAUSTION WHICH COMES UPON A FIGHTER IN EARLY ROUNDS WHEN HE IS ALREADY **TOO TIRED** TO LIFT HIS ARMS OR TAKE ADVANTAGE OF OPENINGS THERE BEFORE HIM YET THE FIGHT IS NOT A THIRD OVER THERE ARE ALL THOSE **ROUNDS TO GO**

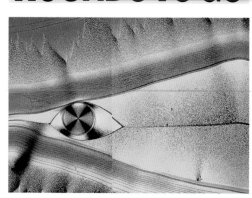

AN EXILE

ozone

maastricht

Santi Caleca, Seoul, 1990.

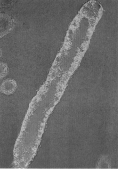

Nonviolence is the basis of the search for truth.

The Indian political and religious leader Mahatma Gandhi (1869-1948) took the first effective steps toward making violence obsolete as a means of political change. Between the two world wars, he used the tactics of ahimsa(nonviolence) and Satyagraha(civil disobedience) to help liberate India from colonial rule. He also invented the concept of the fast as a political weapon. His strategies have been imitated repeatedly in recent history: by the civil rights, antiwar, antinuclear, environmental, and antidiscrimination movements and the participants in the second Russian Revolution in 1991.

It is quite proper to resist and attack a system, but to resist and attack its maker is tantamount to resisting and attacking myself.

For we are all turned with the same brush, and are children of one and the same Creator, and as such the divine powers within us are infinite.

To slight a single human being is to slight those divine powers, and thus to harm not only that being but with him the whole world.

THE HERO
SUPPRESSES
HIS FEARS
AND STEPS INTO
DARKNESS

I like money on the wall. Say you were going to buy a $200,000 painting. I think you should take that money, tie it up, and hang it on the wall. Then when someone visited you, the first thing they would see is the money on the wall.

When I saw my first car as a child, I began running after it. It was a calash-topped sedan, and it was staggering along the narrow village street. I caught up with it and hung onto its rear. When the car stopped, oil dripped to the ground under it. I was deeply stirred. I was intoxicated by the smell of that oil. I put my nose to the ground and drew that smell in

Gee + Chung Design

Principals: Earl Gee,
Fani Chung
Year Founded: 1990
Size of Firm: 4
Key Clients: Apple
Computer, Chronicle Books,
Duty Free Shopping,
Federal Reserve Bank,
Greenleaf Medical, IBM,
Imaginarium, Lucasfilm,
Oracle Corporation,
Smithsonian Institution,
Stanford University,
Sun Microsystems.

38 Bryant Street
Suite 100
San Francisco, CA 94105
415 543 1192

ee + Chung Design has built a reputation for creating dynamic, unexpected and effective solutions for a wide range of two and three-dimensional design challenges. This multi-disciplinary approach is a credit to the strong foundation of Earl Gee, who attended the Art Center College of Design and Fani Chung, who attended Yale University. The success of the firm is guided by a thorough understanding of client objectives and a commitment to making each project the best of its kind. By providing a focus for the client's message through the creation of a visual metaphor and tailoring the message to the client's target audience, Gee + Chung transforms such diverse elements as a logo, brochure, package or tradeshow into a successful and cohesive design program. Dedication to distinctive work provides lasting value, leading the firm into long-term relationships with many clients, including IBM, Chronicle Books and the San Francisco Art Commission. The firm's work has been honored in numerous competitions and recognized by publications including: *Communication Arts*, *Graphis*, *Print* and *I.D.*; and organizations including: AIGA, New York Art Directors Club and San Francisco Art Directors Club. As well, Gee + Chung is represented in the permanent collection of the Library of Congress and has been exhibited internationally.

above
Poster for Greenleaf Medical, Palo Alto, CA. To function as "art" in the offices and clinics of hand surgeons, the poster combines an eclectic selection of hand-related quotes with a variety of hand artifacts, portraying the hand as a universal symbol of time and utility. Art Director/Designer, Earl Gee; photography, Geoffrey Nelson.

right
Poster for the American Institute of Graphic Arts, San Francisco Chapter, CA. Announcing a lecture about the work of Charles and Ray Eames. Their work in furniture, film, exhibitions and graphics was depicted as "points of departure" for the design thought-process. Art Director/Illustrator/Design, Earl Gee.

left
Fani Chung and Earl Gee.
Photography,
Geoffrey Nelson.

right
Logo for the San Francisco
Art Commission, CA. As a
symbol for public artwork
promoting the transit system
on the city's Market Street,
the program's name is integrated into the running,
gesturing figure.
Art Director, Earl Gee;
designers, Earl Gee and
Fani Chung.

right
Trade ad series for Greenleaf
Medical. To express the innovative nature of a computerized
hand-evaluation system for hand
surgeons, a dynamic, modular
compositional organization
allows the individual ads to form
an informational poster with
equal effectiveness.
Art Director/Designer,
Earl Gee; photography,
Geoffrey Nelson.

right
Stationery for the
Community Partnership of
Santa Clara County, San
Jose, CA. The organization
is dedicated to finding fresh
approaches for community
problems. A pattern of
different hands was created
to convey the concepts of
"community" and "diversity."
The color palette identifies
each component, creating a
cohesive system.
Art Director/Designer,
Fani Chung.

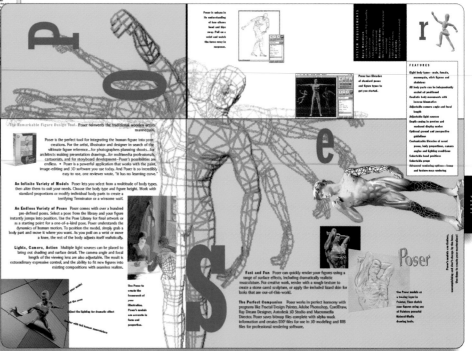

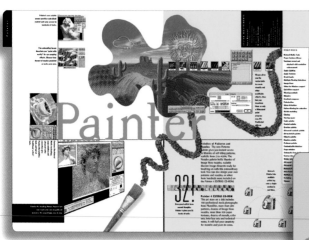

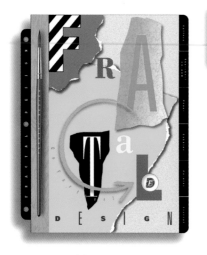

above
Product catalog for Fractal
Design Corporation, Aptos,
CA. A rivet-bound artist's
"idea book" demonstrates
the creative potential of
paint and image-manipula-
tion software that has the
ability to duplicate the
expressive qualities of traditional art media.
Art Director, Earl Gee;
designers, Earl Gee and
Fani Chung.

left
Book design for *Star Wars:
From Concept to Screen to
Collectible*, Chronicle Books,
San Francisco, CA. The
metallic-gold cover utilizes
a positive/negative image of
Darth Vader to symbolize
the "good vs. evil" theme
central to the trilogy.
Art Director, Earl Gee;
designers, Earl Gee and
Fani Chung.

below
Stationery for Xinet, Inc. Berkeley, CA, a Macintosh-Unix server software developer for the electronic pre-press market. The identity system utilizes a restaurant "server" as a metaphor for the company's software while incorporating a typographic system referencing a printer's registration mark. Art Director/Designer, Earl Gee; illustrator, Robert Pastrana.

right
Software package for Xinet, Inc. The restaurant "server" symbolizes software that shares files between two computers. The trapezoidal shape enables the product to stand out in the retail environment and on the user's shelf. Art Directors/Designers, Earl Gee and Fani Chung; illustrator, Robert Pastrana.

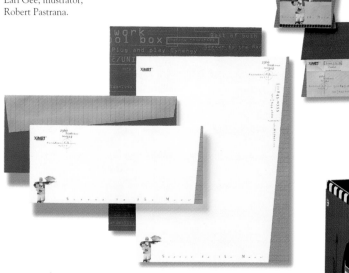

below
Package for Imaginarium, Walnut Creek, CA. For a retail toy chain's own brand of hoppity-hop ball, the concept of fun is expressed by integrating the child and product into the logotype itself. The brightly-colored box panels offer a multitude of in-store display possibilities. Art Director/Illustrator/Design, Earl Gee; photography, Sandra Frank.

right
Software package for Quorum Software Systems, Inc., Menlo Park, CA. Metallic copper and embossed ribbing were used to project an upscale positioning for a program that enables Macintosh software to run on high-powered RISC work stations. Art Directors/Designers, Earl Gee and Fani Chung; illustrator, John Mattos.

left and below
Tradeshow exhibit for Chronicle Books, San Francisco, CA. The American Booksellers Association booth incorporates a gear, ladder, staircase and human figure as metaphors connotating work, progress, attainment and humanity. The natural wood and aluminum set the stage to highlight Chronicle's colorful collection.
Art Director/Designer, Earl Gee; fabrication, Barr Exhibits.

left
Logo for 3-D Motion, San Francisco, CA. A glowing "beacon" was used to represent a firm that specializes in computer generated animation, architectural models and three-dimensional "fly-bys."
Art Director/Designer, Fani Chung.

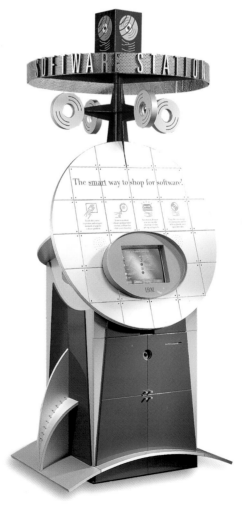

left
Interactive kiosk for IBM Corporation, San Francisco, CA. This "software vending machine" offering electronic delivery on-demand via satellite transmission utilizes space-station and satellite references to create a striking, sculptural, in-store presence.
Art Director/Designer, Earl Gee; fabrication, Hood Exhibits.

Greteman Group

Principal: Sonia Greteman
Year Founded: 1989
Primary Clients: Learjet,
Mooney Aircraft, Kansas
Health Foundation,
Duffens Optical, Center for
the Arts, Galichia Medical
Group, Wichita Industries
& Services for the Blind,
Sierra Suites Hotel,
Summerfield Suites Hotel,
Brite Voice Systems, Bank
of Kansas, Thermos.

142 North Mosley
Wichita, KS 67202
316.263.1004
www.gretemangroup.com

reteman Group cultivates a reputation for concept-oriented design delivered with honesty and strength. Rooted in the spirit of the grasslands, the firm of eight explores the past and present to create design solutions for tomorrow. Creating works of distinctive style and beauty, its designers transform concepts into visual communication that speaks to the heart as well as the mind. And, above all, accomplishes results. Greteman Group and clients work together as a team, setting goals and devising strategies. Whether it's a corporate identity or interactive multimedia, they abandon the comfort zone to develop adventurous design solutions that are grounded, yet boundless.

below left
Open house invitation and
logo for Galichia Medical
Group, Wichita, KS.
Celebrates the company's
10th anniversary by mark-
ing each year's milestone
on an ascending stairway.
Designers, Sonia Greteman
and James Strange.

above and below
Annual report for Kansas
Health Foundation,
Wichita, KS. Emphasizes
a strong Kansas feeling
through assemblages
incorporating vintage photos, antique notions and
native flora.
Designer/Illustrator,
Sonia Greteman.

left
Principal Sonia Greteman.
Photography, Ron Berg.

right
Logo design for
Greteman Group.
Designers, Sonia Greteman
and James Strange.

far right
Logo design for
Planet Hair.
Designer, Sonia Greteman.

left
Cookbook for Junior
League of Wichita, KS,
Women of Great Taste.
Tongue-in-cheek illustrations
humorously salute women
and their zest for food.
Designers, Sonia Greteman
and James Strange;
illustrator, Greteman.

right
Capabilities brochure for
Learjet, Wichita, KS.
Showcases the advantages
of the Learjet 60, posi-
tioning it as the consum-
mate transcontinental
business jet.
Designers, Sonia Greteman
and James Strange;
photography, Paul Bowen.

Learjet 60

left
Logo design for GreenAcres,
a natural foods market,
Wichita, KS.
Designer, Sonia Greteman.

below
Direct mail, stationery
and sack for GreenAcres.
Designers, Sonia Greteman,
James Strange and
Karen Hogan.

far left
Exterior signage and
menu for Oaxaca Grill, a
fine restaurant featuring
Meso American cuisine,
Wichita, KS.
Designers, Sonia Greteman,
Craig Tomson, Jo Quillin
and Chris Parks.

far left
Logo design for Kansas Health Foundation, a philanthropic organization that finances programs for the long-term betterment of public health, Wichita, KS. Designers, Sonia Greteman and James Strange.

left
Logo design for Perfectly Round Productions, a film and video production house, Wichita, KS. Designer, Sonia Greteman.

above
Development poster for black rhino conservation, Ngare Sergoi Rhino Sanctuary, Kenya, Africa. Designers, Sonia Greteman and Jeanette Palkowetz; illustrator, Greteman.

above right
Packaging for Tutteri's Pasta, Kansas City, MO. Evokes an Old World feeling of pasta lovingly and painstakingly made by hand. Designer/Illustrator, Sonia Greteman.

right
Package design for Hayes Forest Products, "Flower & Herb Garden," Wichita, KS. Designers, Sonia Greteman and James Strange; illustrators, Greteman and C.B. Mordan.

right
Logo design for Brite Voice
Systems; telecommunica-
tions products, systems and
services, Wichita, KS.
Designer, James Strange

far right
Logo design for Winning
Visions, an ophthalmology
marketing group,
Wichita, KS.
Designer, Sonia Greteman.

above
Exterior signage for Wichita
Racquet Club, a health and
fitness center, Wichita, KS.
Designer, Sonia Greteman.

below
Exterior signage for
MotorWorks auto repair,
Wichita, KS. Back light-
ing and a turning gear cre-
ate drama and interest.
Designer, Sonia Greteman.

above
Game design for Kansas
LEAN, "Jack Sprat's
Table" provides fun while
teaching children about
the food pyramid and how
to budget their fat intake.
Designer, Sonia Greteman;
illustrators, Greteman and
Shawn Money.

right
Cover design for brochure
announcing an anti-violence
motivational lecture by the
Rev. Jesse Jackson targeted
to high-school students,
Koch Crime Commission,
Wichita, KS.
Designers, Sonia Greteman
and James Strange.

right
Logo design for Leadership Wichita, a community leadership-building program sponsored by the Wichita Area Chamber of Commerce. Designer, Sonia Greteman.

far right
Logo design for Jake's Attic, a children's science show on television targeted to grades K-5, Wichita, KS. Designer, Sonia Greteman.

below
Capabilities brochure for PrintMaster, an offset lithographer, Wichita, KS. Designers, Sonia Greteman, James Strange, Bill Gardner and Karen Hogan; illustrator, Greteman.

bottom
World Wide Web home page design for Greteman Group. Designers, Sonia Greteman, Craig Tomson and Todd Gimlin; illustrator, Greteman.

above
Poster for the nation's largest Bowl for Kids' Sake, Big Brothers & Sisters of Sedgwick County, Wichita. KS. Designers, Sonia Greteman and James Strange.

left
Christmas card for Aspen Traders, a nature-inspired clothing store, Wichita, KS. Designer, Sonia Greteman.

The Grillo Group, Inc.

Principal: Maria L. Grillo
Year Founded: 1996
Size of Firm: 4
Key Clients: American
Medical Association,
Chicago Symphony
Orchestra, Citicorp Diners
Club Inc., City of Chicago
Department of Planning
and Development, Design
Industry Foundation for
AIDS (DIFFA), Florian
Architects, Follet
Corporation: Custom
Academic Publishing
Company (CAPCO),
Mohawk Paper Mills, Inc.;

Museum of Science and
Industry, Rehabilitation
Institute of Chicago, The
Robert Wood Johnson
Foundation, The University
of Chicago Graduate
School of Business.

55 East Washington Street
Suite 1030
Chicago, IL 60602
312 782 2363

The Grillo Group is fortunate to have many loyal clients who take their market perception seriously. The firm's relationships are based on trust, openness, flexibility and follow-through to create work both client and designer can stand behind. "Our clients ask us to help them reach their audiences—to inform, motivate and remind them—through content, theme, text and imagery with focus and emotional impact," says Maria Grillo, principal of The Grillo Group. "We take the product message and the needs of the target audience to heart. Our use of style, to promote rather than replace message content, is what clients tell us brings them back." Grillo is an instructor of design at The School of the Art Institute of Chicago and a visiting instructor at Syracuse University's Independent Study Master of Arts Program. She also judges numerous design competitions and lectures throughout the country.

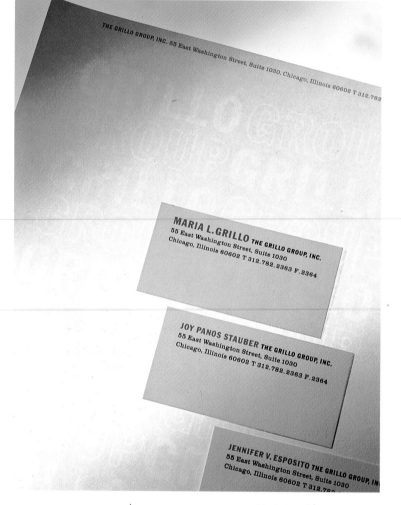

above
Identity and stationery applications for The Grillo Group, Inc. "The repeated company name on the stationery acts as a subtle but constant reminder of who we are and how we work," says Grillo.
Designers, Maria Grillo and Joy Panos Stauber.

opposite page right
Identity and promotional materials for Carr Cialdella Photography, Kalamazoo, MI, created for an existing and prospective client base of art directors, designers, corporate communications managers and architects. Survey results from past, current and potential clients revealed detailed and conclusive audience characteristics, which provided strong direction for designers.
Designers, Maria Grillo and Joy Panos Stauber; survey research and analysis, Charles G Kratz; text, The Grillo Group.

left
Maria Grillo of The Grillo
Group, Inc. outside her
office at the corner of
Washington and Wabash
in Chicago.

FOR
CENTURIES
THE YEAR 2000
HAS STOOD FOR
THE FUTURE AND
WHAT WE SHALL
MAKE OF
IT.

soon that future will be here.

The Billennium®
The Official Celebration of the Year 2000™

The Year 2000

will be the defining moment of our lifetime. This monumental psychological and historical turning point will be inescapable, with people around the world caught up in the need to celebrate the inherent drama of the most significant moment in history.

A moment that is approaching rapidly.

This excitement will be captured and expressed by The Billennium®, a once-in-a-lifetime series of global media events and products, celebrating the world's accomplishments over the past 2000 years and culminating with one of the greatest celebrations in history.

The Billennium® celebration is the only globally registered trademark related to the coming millennium. Reminiscent of other successful internationally recognized celebrations such as the Bicentennials in the United States, France and Australia, The Billennium incorporates the best from the past, present and future. More than just a brief moment in time, The Billennium celebration is a combination of entertainment, education and exclusive sponsorship opportunities for select companies.

The Billennium is...

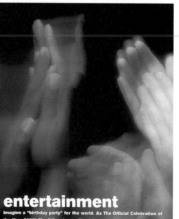

entertainment
Imagine a "birthday party" for the world. As The Official Celebration of the Year 2000, The Billennium® will celebrate mankind's creative spirit through proprietary entertainment, arts and cultural events, products and media vehicles. Each will create memories that last a lifetime.

education
With Billennium "Time for Discovery"™ educational products and The Billennium Time Capsule, a historical and cultural discovery center, the world will explore the ideas of the last 2000 years, while being inspired to achieve accomplishments for the next millennium.

global sponsorships
The Year 2000 is the marketing opportunity of the millennium. As The Official Celebration of the Year 2000, The Billennium® offers select companies the benefits of exclusive sponsorship and access to a vast and valuable global audience.

be a part of it.

It's just a few ticks of the clock away.
Being a part of The Billennium®, The Official Celebration of the Year 2000, needs to start now. For more information, call 312.327.2000. Fax 312.327.1999. Send e-mail to billennium@aol.com. Or visit our home page at www.billennium.com.

The Billennium®
The Official Celebration of the Year 2000™

opposite page left
Brochure and website for The Mitten Group, Inc.; Chicago, IL. To fully communicate the drama, excitement and anticipation associated with the turn of the century, the brochure introduces The Billennium® as "The Official Celebration of the Year 2000" to potential corporate and enter-tainment industry sponsors. The website increases awareness and invites people "to be a part of it." Designers, Maria Grillo, Joy Panos Stauber and Tim Bruce; text, Mark Mitten and Peter Zapf; photography, Peter Frahm.

right
One of a series of posters for Posted Communications, Chicago, IL. The posters enable businesses to comply with a range of legal, health and policy issues, and to visually set itself apart in the world of mass market informational and motivational posters. Each series is meant to complement other posters in the product line, providing customers a variety of options. Designers, Maria Grillo and Jennifer Wiess; text, Grillo and Anne E. Celano; photography, Peter Frahm.

smoke free environment

second hand smoke doesn't discriminate

left
Coffee table book documenting the working process of two brothers, *Zhou Bros In the Studio*, Oxford University Press, New York, NY. Its concept is based on the idea of "two individual parts creating one"; an analogy to the artists' relationship as brothers working together, as well as their individual but complementing viewpoints, methods and perceptions which create a unified result. Designers, Maria Grillo and Michael Anderson; text, Anderson; photography, Steven E. Gross.

top left
Identity and promotional
materials for Gleason,
McGuire & Schreffler
Attorneys at Law, Chicago,
IL. The identity/monogram
was designed to be under-
stated—same color on
color. The monogram format
was used to reference a
familiar analogy for quality
and good taste; red was
chosen to address the strong
personalities of the partners.
Designers, Maria Grillo
and Jennifer Wiess; text,
Ted Stoik; photography,
François Robert.

left
Identity materials for Florian
Architects, a nationally
known and recognized firm,
Chicago, IL. To demonstrate
the firm's understanding of
the embodiment of function,
the format was based on the
use of a piece of letterhead
and the name of the firm.
The "F" printed on the
reverse of the letterhead
marks a 1-inch letter mar-
gin as well as the location
of folds for mailing in a
standard #10 envelope. The
"F" also acts as a reference
to division of space and volume in architecture.
Designers, Maria Grillo and
Tim Bruce.

above
Direct mail campaign for
Citicorp Diners Club Inc.,
Chicago, IL. The campaign
included postcards and
statement inserts targeted
at current and potential
Corporate Cardmembers.
The format of each execu-
tion addresses product benefits through literal examples of card use; questions
are focused on personal
Cardmembers needs that
card benefits can fulfill.
Designers, Maria Grillo
and Joy Panos Stauber; text,
LoCurto and Associates.

Brochure and application materials for The University of Chicago Graduate School of Business Executive M.B.A. Program, Chicago and Barcelona. Emotionally packed photos and highly structured typography illustrate the intensity of the program. Case studies were used to communicate the program's impact on students and their corporations. Individual experiences and actual corporate projects that were achieved as a direct result of participation in the program were included. Designers, Maria Grillo and Joy Panos Stauber; text, Patricia Nedeau (Director of Publications for the Graduate School of Business); printing, Bruce Offset; photography, Loren Santow.

Jessica Helfand Studio, Ltd.

Principal: Jessica Helfand
Year Founded: 1994
Size of Firm: 3
Key Clients: American
Lawyer Media, AT&T,
Champion International
Corporation, Discovery
Communications, Dow
Jones Information Systems,
The New York Times,
Philadelphia Museum of Art.

214 Sullivan Street
Suite 6C
New York, NY 10012
212 388 1863
www.jhstudio.com

essica Helfand Studio is a small design consultancy that concentrates on editorial design and the development of new models for new media. In an effort to better define and articulate the impact of technology on the design professions, Jessica Helfand is a contributing editor to both *Eye* and *I.D.* magazines, and has been a visiting lecturer in interaction design at The Cooper Union and New York University's Program in Interactive Telecommunications. Her focus and that of her studio lies in mapping a new kind of editorial process for the strategic development of electronic media, including CD-ROMs, internet web sites, and theoretical projects that introduce alternative conceptual paradigms for communication design.

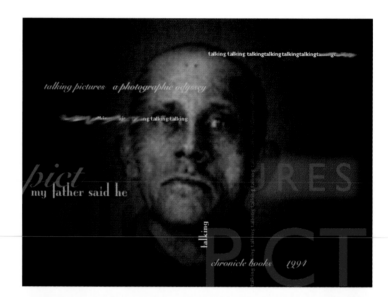

left
Navigational toolbar for Champion International Corporation's website, Stamford, CT. The clickable letterforms of the logo are used to denote the eight categorical subdivisions within the site.
Creative Director, Jessica Helfand; designers, Michelle Mierzwa and Peter Cho.

above
Two screens from the opening sequence for *Talking Pictures*, a CD-ROM to accompany the book and exhibition by the same name, for Chronicle Books, San Francisco, CA. A sequence of mug shots taken at Auschwitz erode as the type and voice/over become more prominent.
Art Director, Jessica Helfand; producers; Carole Kismaric, Marvin Heiferman.

left
Jessica Helfand.
Photography,
Ray Charles White.

below
Dust jacket for a bibliography
of the work of Paul Auster,
Designer, Jessica Helfand;
photography, Victor
Schrager; publisher, William
Drenttel New York.

below right
Illustration for Philadelphia
Inquirer Magazine, PA. The
story is about an apartment
dweller who continues to
receive mail intended for a
former occupant.
Illustrator, Jessica Helfand

below
The Birthday Grid, a
theoretical proposal for a
birth announcement series
that uses an information
matrix to merge personal
and historical data.
Designer, Jessica Helfand

Paul Auster

A COMPREHENSIVE BIBLIOGRAPHIC CHECKLIST
OF PUBLISHED WORKS 1968–1994

March	21	1960	6:30 am
the third month of the year, containing thirty-one days; three is the heavenly number, and it represents the soul, multiplicity, growth and creativity	ten times two plus one, noted often as XXI	Harper Lee writes *To Kill a Mockingbird*	the weather report says fair and cool, high 43, low 28
	a multiple of three (3x7)	John F. Kennedy is elected President	on television, <u>Sunrise Semester</u> was on CBS. Scheduled: Psychology S-1: Motivation; on NBC, <u>Continental Classroom</u> offered Chemistry: *The Chemical Literature* (in living color); Dave Garroway and the Today show came on at 7:00. Dave's guests included piano satirist and singer Richard Hayes, Florence henderson and Frank Blair
to walk with a regular and measured tread, as soldiers; advance in step in an organized body; to walk in a stately or in a deliberate manner; to proceed or to advance; to cause to march; the act or the course of marching; also, a piece of music with a rhythm suited to accompany the act of marching	the first day of the third week of the month, and in this month, the cusp between Aries and Pisces on the Zodiac calendar	Oscar Hammerstein II dies at the age of 65	
	Johann Sebastian Bach, born 21.3 1685. (If 1685 is added to 1960 the total, 3645, is also a multiple of 3 (3x1215)	*Fiorello!* wins the Pulitzer prize for drama	
		Bobby Fischer, age 16, wins the U.S. chess championship	
	drinking age in certain states	the Pittsburgh Pirates beat the New York Yankees 4-3 in the 57th World Series	
a tract of land along a border of a country; frontier; the border district between England and Scotland	a card game		I was born at Albert Einstein medical center in Philadelphia

7 lbs., 6 ounces |

below and opposite page
Representative screens from the studio's website, a theoretical project that focuses on reconsidering word/image relationships to tell old stories in new ways. The site takes its cue from a series of photographs from an album found in an antique store in Kansas City, all taken between 1911 and 1932. With these photographs as a point of departure, stories were generated linking people and events—both factual and fictional—to one another and to the photographic environment they share. "This project gives renewed life to a document long forgotten, and suggests a new model for electronic publishing that examines the way we visualize biography, the way we contextualize history, and the way we address the perpetually changing roles of audience and author." Creative Director, Jessica Helfand; producer, Barbara Genova; designers, Michelle Mierzwa, Irwin Chen, Jessica Safran and Peter Cho.

[taken in france]

Me *Oh*

A Breath

*So*There

Another

Southern

Sweet Like a

crow

Just Visiting

692

The Dreams Remain

It went on for a long time. Seven years.
When it began we were ten. And then
we were twelve. Then thirteen.

Then fourteen, fifteen.

Then sixteen, seventeen.

It lasted all that age, seven years.

And then finally hope was given up.
Abandoned. *Abandoned.*
to her friends, her lovers,
Like the struggles against the sea.
her acquaintances, everybody.
Very early in my life it was already too late.
It was as if she drew a
My ageing was very sudden.
glittering rope of knowledge
I've heard of the way time can suddenly
out of the sea of darkness,
accelerate on people
drew and drew it out of the
when they're going through the most
fathomless depths of the past,
youthful and highly esteemed
and still it did not come to an end
stages of life.
there was no end to it -
I knew I was right.
she must haul and haul
I knew one day time would
at the rope of glittering consciousness
slow down
till she was weary, aching, exhausted
and take its normal course.

She was exhausted, wearied ...
conscious of everything —
her childhood, her girlhood,
all the forgotten incidents,
all the unrealised influences and
all the happenings
she had not understood.

pertaining to herself, to her family,

and fit to break ...

and fit to break ...

I see now why I wanted my wife to come back.
I wonder if you can advise me.
It was because of what she had made me into.
I've been having a bit of a rough time
We had not been alone again for fifteen minutes
with this clock.
Before I felt, and still more acutely -
The tick's been keeping me up.
Indeed, acutely, perhaps, for the first time,
The trouble is I'm not all that convinced
The whole oppression, the unreality
it was the clock.
Of the role she had always imposed upon me
I mean, there are lots of things
With the obstinate, unconscious,
which tick in the night,
subhuman strength that some women have.
don't you find that?
Without her, it was vacancy.
All sorts of objects which, in the day, Tick.
When I thought she had left me, I began to
you couldn't call anything but
d i s s o l v e , to cease to exist. That Tick.
commonplace. They give you no trouble.
was what she had done to me!
But in the night any one of Tick.
I cannot live with her - that is now intolerable;
a number of them
I cannot live without her, because she has
is liable to start letting out
made me incapable of having any
a bit of a tick.
existence of my own. That is what she has
Tick.
done to me in five years together!

She has made the world a place I cannot live in
Tick.
Except on her terms. I must be alone
Tick.
but not in the same world ...
Tick.

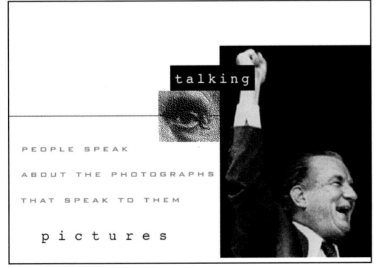

opposite page/top
Unpublished typographic studies for the redesign of *Poetry in Motion*, a CD-ROM published by The Voyager, New York, NY. Designer, Jessica Helfand.

opposite page/bottom
Representative frames from ... *And Fit to Break*, an unpublished CD-ROM proposal based on the spontaneous narrative created by the simultaneous presence of two disparate texts. Designer, Jessica Helfand.

above
Representative screen from a proposed redesign for a website for *Prodigy*, New York, NY. Art Director/Designer, Jessica Helfand.

left
Opening screen from promotional teaser for *Talking Pictures*, an unpublished CD-ROM based on the book and exhibition by the same title, for Chronicle Books, San Francisco, CA. Art Director/Designer, Jessica Helfand.

Kiku Obata & Company

Principal: Kiku Obata
Year Founded: 1977
Size of Firm: 44
Key Clients: American Multi-Cinema, Barnes & Noble, BJC Health System, DeBartolo Properties, The Florida Aquarium, Great Lakes Science Center, Missouri Botanical Garden, Renault, Roto-Rooter, Simon Properties Group, Southwestern Bell, Special Olympics International.

5585 Pershing Avenue
Suite 240
St. Louis, MO 63112
314 361 3110

(K)iku Obata & Company specializes in environmental and print graphics, and retail store design. Excellence in research, programming, concepts, design and implementation has consistently produced effective results for clients. The firm's work in environmental graphics directs people in, through, and out of some of the nation's leading malls, sports facilities and assembly centers; its design of retail stores involves customers on an emotional and physical level, transforming shopping into an entertaining experience; its print programs—corporate identities, annual reports, brochures, advertising campaigns, logos and invitations—communicate ideas effectively without imposing a particular style of design. All of these components comprise Kiku Obata & Company's success and ensure the quality and timelessness of the firm's work.

above
Invitation for the California Academy of Sciences' 1994 annual ball, San Francisco, CA. Using pop-out shapes and illustrations to grab attention, the invitation was so well received that the caterers used it in designing their food displays. Designer, Amy Knopf; illustrator, Rich Nelson.

right
Poster for Circus Flora, St. Louis, MO. To promote the traveling circus, the identity and graphics included a poster and wine bottle labels (not shown). Designer/Illustrator, Ed Mantels-Seeker.

left
Advertising campaign for Plaza Frontenac, St. Louis, MO, an upscale mall that recently underwent a major renovation. Art Director/Designer, Pam Bliss; designer, John Scheffel; photography, Gregg Goldman (fashion), and David Stradal (still); illustrator, Brian Otto; copywriters, Carole Jerome and Sara Harrell.

left
Kiku Obata.

below
Logo for Planet Comics, Lake Grove, NY, one component of an identity for a new chain of retail stores selling comic books and video games. The rocket ship recalls the days when comic books became popular. Designer/Illustrator, Rich Nelson.

Community School

TheHernia Institute:

Beacon Health Care

below
Identity, name and logo development, letterhead system and promotional/marketing materials for Communications by Proxy, Annapolis, MD, a new global communications company. Art Directors, Rich Nelson, and Jim Datema; designer, Rich Nelson; copywriter, Carole Jerome.

above
(left to right)
Logo for the Community School, St. Louis, MO. The illustration conveys a childlike, yet sophisticated image for a private grade school, and has the versatility to be reproduced many different ways. Designer, Amy Knopf; illustrator, Sara Love.

Logo for The Hernia Institute, St. Louis, MO. The logo focuses on benefits of treatment (the ability to move without pain), rather than on the condition of the hernia. Designer, Ed Mantels-Seeker.

Logo for Beacon Health Care, St. Louis, MO, anchoring a complete identity program for 16 merging medical practices. The logo represents "a point of light and direction in an ever-changing healthcare environment." Designer, Jim Datema; illustrator, Rich Nelson.

above
(top to bottom)
Capabilities book for HOK Architects, St. Louis, MO. Designer, Rich Nelson; photography, various.

Annual report for Barnes & Noble, New York, NY. A fictitious character was created to take the reader on a tour of an imaginary bookstore. Designer, Joseph Floresca; copywriters, Sara Harrell and Maira Kalman, illustrator, Kalman.

Annual report for Anheuser-Busch Employees Credit Union (ABECU), St. Louis, MO. The annual report focuses on keeping up with technological advancements in the industry while developing and maintaining customer relationships. Designer, Kathleen Robert; copywriter, Sara Harrell; photography, Gregg Goldman.

above

Identity and store design for P.B. Pages, Bloomington, MN, a division of Barnes & Noble. The concept, name identity, store design, visual merchandising, fixtures and signage were created for a children's bookstore in the Mall of America. The design highlights the qualities of books: knowledge, adventure, fantasy and fun.

Design team: Kiku Obata, James Keane AIA, Idie McGinty, Tim McGinty AIA, Theresa Henrekin, Jane McNeely, Amy Knopf and Pam Bliss; photography, Greg Hursley; fixture fabricator, Design Fabricators, Inc.

left and above

Store design and identity for B. Dalton Bookseller, a division of Barnes & Noble. The overall concept, name development, identity, visual merchandising, signage and promotional materials were designed specifically for the mall customer who is motivated mainly by impulse and entertainment.

Design team: Kiku Obata, James Keane AIA, Jane McNeely, Pam Bliss, Theresa Henrekin, Tim McGinty AIA and Idie McGinty; photography, Cheryl Pendleton.

below and right
Candy store identity, name and design for Help Ur Self, Inc., Pittsburgh, PA. Designers created a fictitious candy company adding "corporate touches" throughout the store, such as a roll-top desk, chandeliers and the company logo inlaid into the floor.
Design team: Kiku Obata, James Keane AIA, Jane McNeely, Sylvia Teng, Tim McGinty AIA, and Idie McGinty; photography, Ed Massery.

left and below
Store design for Big Future, Inc., St. Louis, MO. The design objective was to create a unified design, including concept, identity, signage, store design and interactive exhibits that appealed to school-age children and their parents.
Design team: Kiku Obata, Gen Obata, Rich Nelson, Tim McGinty AIA, Jane McNeely, James Keane AIA and Theresa Henrekin; photography, Alise O'Brien.

above and right
Store design and identity for Oilily's Somerset Collection, Troy, MI. Store fixtures allude to the imported nature of merchandise offered by Oilily, a women and children's clothier headquartered in the Netherlands.

Design team: Kiku Obata, Gen Obata, Rich Nelson, Tim McGinty AIA, Jane McNeely, James Keane AIA and Theresa Henrekin; photography, Balthazar Korab.

above and right
Comprehensive exterior and interior environmental graphics program, including logo, advertising and sponsorship programs for Coors Field, Denver, CO. The graphics reflect industrial styles and western themes, adding a nostalgic regionalism to the baseball stadium. Design team: Kiku Obata, Todd Mayberry, Tim McGinty AIA, Kay Pangraze, Teresa O'Brien, Heather Testa, and Beth Mayberry; photography, Gary Quesada.

left
Mall of America's environmental graphics and signage for Melvin Simon and Associates, Indianapolis, IN. Design team: Kiku Obata, Idie McGinty, Tim McGinty AIA, Kay Pangraze, Heather Testa, Pam Bliss, Rich Nelson, Jane McNeely, Theresa Henrekin, Amy Knopf, Teresa Norton-Young and Ed Mantels-Seeker; photography, Greg Hursley; signage fabricators, Cornelius Architectural Products; sign services, Andco Industries Corp., and Nordquist Sign Co.

left and below left
Environmental graphics for
the St. Louis Science Center.
The wayfinding system was
designed, built and installed
in nine months and within
an extremely tight budget.
Design team: Kiku Obata,
Heather Testa, Kay Pangraze,
Rich Nelson and Teresa
O'Brien; photography, Greg
Hursley; sign fabricators,
Engravings Unlimited,
Cherokee Sales, Universal
Sign Systems, Ferger Design
and Nordquist Sign Co.

below
Signage, theme graphics,
seating bowl theme and
color selection for a new
multi-purpose sports and
entertainment complex for
Kiel Center Partners,
St. Louis, MO.
Design team: Kiku Obata,
Heather Testa, Kay Pangraze,
Tim McGinty AIA, Patty
LaTour, Jeanna Stoll and
Amy Knopf; photography,
Cheryl Pendleton and
Jon Miller.

left and below
Theater restoration,
lighting, graphics and
signage for an historic arts
and entertainment district
managed by Grand Center,
St. Louis, MO.
Design team: Heather
Testa, John Scheffel, Tim
McGinty AIA and Jane
McNeely; photography,
Balthazar Korab; sign fabri-
cators, Engravings
Unlimited, Warren Signs,
Star Signs, Mon-Clair
Signs Inc.; installation,
Signcrafters Inc.

Looking

Principals: John Clark,
Marianne Thompson,
Carol Newsom
Year Founded: 1990
Size of Firm: 6
Key Clients: American
Stores Company,
Architectural Response
Kollection, Capri/Omega
Lighting, Le Groupe Equus,
Martin/Brattrud, Plan Hold
International, Progress
Lighting, Ribot, Standard
Pacific Corp., UCLA.

660 South Avenue 21
Los Angeles, CA 90031
213 227 1450

Looking is an active verb. The firm's primary objective is to create and develop client identities with a long-term dedication to the idea of working *with*—as opposed to *for them*. "We have learned," says Looking's founder John Clark, "that continuous communication is the surest way to build effective solutions to our clients' needs." With approximately 90 percent of its work created within such relationships, the firm considers learning its clients' businesses a top priority in the total flow of communication that is, for Looking, the design process. In many ways, Looking sees much of its work as a question of identity development. As a key to marketing value and quality, the firm understands that at the core the design process is a diligent commitment to the highest level of communication. Within these parameters, Looking's projects are as diverse as trademarks, annual reports and literature systems, identities for events, exhibits, packaging and interactive media.

above
Poster to protest the baseball strike for Baseball Fans Everywhere. The poster captures and expresses the frustration of true baseball fans, and at how financial interests had perverted and undone the sport. The solution attempts a loving, yet critical look at the symbol of our national pastime. Designers, John Clark and Donald Miller.

left
From left: Jennifer Bressler,
John Clark, Carol Newsom,
Donna Fischer, Gary Wong
and Marianne Thompson.
Photography,
Marshal Safron.

right
Self promotional New Year's
greeting. The "Looking
Glasses" are created from
cast aluminum to create
unbreakable glasses.
Designer, John Clark.

below
Promotional poster and
book cover for Marsilio
Publishers, New York, NY.
The integration of face and
typography forms a single
expression, capturing the
spirit of the writer and book.
Designers, John Clark and
Marianne Thompson.

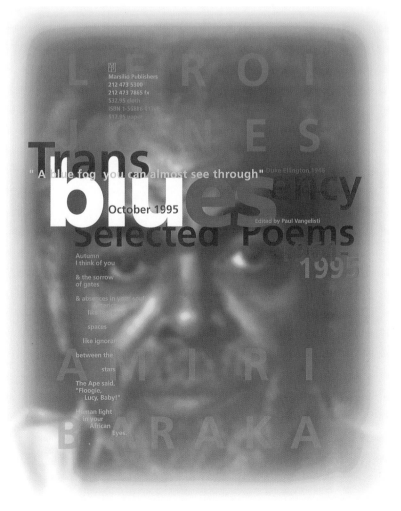

left and above
Identity and promotional
materials for triennial
international poetry event
for the Department of
Italian, UCLA, Los Angeles,
CA. To create a memorable
and unified identity, as well
as symbolize the location
of the event, a visual representation of an orange (vs.
The Big Apple) was used.
Designer, John Clark.

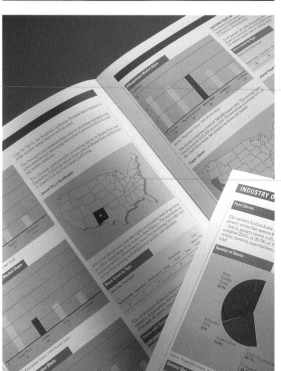

above and above right
Annual reports and fact
book for American Stores
Company, Salt Lake City,
UT. The annual reports
respond to specific company
management objectives,
while maintaining a consistent approach to their communications. The fact book
provides a quick reference
to all vital company statistics.
Designers/annual report,
John Clark, Donna Fischer,
Melissa Hertz, Paul Langland
and Marianne Thompson.
Designers/fact book, John
Clark, Donna Fischer and
Laurent Tschumy.

right
Introductory brochure to
a new consulting program
for Price Waterhouse,
Los Angeles, CA. Taking
place of much of the text,
strong visual metaphors were
used to explain the program.
Designer, John Clark.

above
Product presentation and revised company positioning for Omega Lighting, Los Angeles, CA. It includes sophisticated application and technical information to establish it as a high-end company within the industry of architectural commercial lighting. Designers, John Clark, Carol Newsom and Donna Fischer.

left and above left
Identity for Plan Hold Corporation, Irvine, CA. The identity expresses the common thread through all branches of the company. Designers, John Clark and Laurent Tschumy.

left and above left
Identity for Heuristic
Development Group, Pacific
Palisades, CA. The health
system was based around a
"smart card," a personal
encoded card used at the
health club's computerized
kiosk. It gives updated health
and workout information
onscreen or printed out.
Shown are the forms printed
out from the computer and
a screen image from the
kiosk. Intended for large
corporations that have in-
house health clubs, the
identity captures both the
fitness and technological
aspects of the company
appropriate to the health
industry.
Designers, John Clark and
Donna Fischer.

right
Newsletter for Design ARC, Santa Barbara, CA. It presents a full range of editorial, news and project developments on a quarterly basis. Designer, Donna Fischer.

bottom
Annual report for the College of Neglected Science, Los Angeles, CA. Titled *Ribot 3*, it presents poetry, prose and art from an international community. The publication is a compact format, 'subversive' in character, and in keeping with the nature of the client. Design team: Looking.

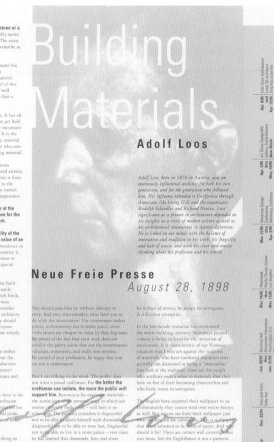

Building Materials

Adolf Loos

Which is worth more, a kilogram of stone or a kilogram of gold? The question probably seems ridiculous. But only to the merchant. The artist will answer: All materials are equally valuable as far as I am concerned.

The artist has only one ambition: to master his material in such a way that his work is independent of the value of the raw material. Our architects, however, have not heard of this ambition. For them, a square meter of wall surface out of granite is more valuable than a square meter out of plaster.

But granite in and of itself is worthless. It lies all around outside in the fields; anyone can get hold of it. It forms whole mountains, whole mountain ranges, which one has only to dig up. It is the most common stone, the most ordinary material that we know. And yet there are people who consider granite our most precious building material.

These people say "material" but they mean "work." Human labor, technical skill, and artistry. For granite demands much work to wrest it from the mountains, much work to bring it to the designated location, work to give it the correct form and to endow it with a pleasing appearance by cutting and polishing. **Our hearts beat with reverential awe at the sight of the polished granite wall. Awe for the material? No, awe for the human work.**

It is not just the quantity, but the quality of the work performed that determines the value of an object. We live in a time that gives precedence to the quantity of work performed. For quantity is easily controlled, it is immediately obvious to anyone and demands no skilled eye or special knowledge.

It was not always this way. Formerly one built with the materials that were the most easily obtainable. In some regions this was with brick, in some with stone; in some the walls were stuccoed. Did those who used stucco consider themselves somewhat inferior to those architects who built in stone? Of course not, why should they have? The idea did not occur to anyone. If there were quarries in the vicinity, one simply built out of stone.

Today it is not the artist who rules, but rather the day laborer, not the creative idea, but the working hours. But any amount of production time costs money. And if one has no money? Then one begins to fake the working hours and to imitate materials.

The reverence for the quantity of work done is the most fearsome enemy that the crafts profession has. For it results in imitation. And imitation has demoralized a large part of our crafts. All pride, all handicraft spirit have fled. A spirit of utter degradation pervades.

It is no surprise that this profession is doing so badly. Such people cannot help but do badly. Carpenter, be proud that you are a carpenter! It is the stuccoworker who makes ornaments.

Neue Freie Presse
August 28, 1898

You should pass him by without jealousy or envy. And you, stuccoworker, what have you to do with the stonemason? The stonemason makes joints, unfortunately has to make joints, since little stones are cheaper to come by than big ones. Be proud of the fact that your work does not exhibit the paltry joints that cut the stonemason's columns, ornaments, and walls into sections. Be proud of your profession, be happy that you are not a stonemason!

But I am talking to the wind. The public does not want a proud craftsman. **For the better the craftsman can imitate, the more the public will support him.** Reverences for expensive materials — the surest sign of the parvenu crops in which our nation currently finds itself — will have it no other way. The parvenu considers it disgraceful not to be able to adorn himself with diamonds, disgraceful not to be able to wear furs, disgraceful not to be able to live in a stone palace – ever since he has learned that diamonds, furs, and stone palaces cost a great deal of money. He does not know that the lack of diamonds, furs, and stone facades has no effect on elegance. Therefore, since he is short of money, he grasps for surrogates. A ridiculous enterprise.

In the last decade imitation has dominated the entire building industry. Nowadays poured cement is being utilized for the imitation of stuccowork. It is characteristic of our Viennese situation that I who am against the violation of materials, who have combated imitation energetically, am dismissed as being a "materialist." Just look at the sophistry: these are the people who attribute such a value to materials that they have no fear of their becoming characterless and who freely resort to surrogates.

The English have exported their wallpaper to us. Unfortunately they cannot send over entire houses as well. But we can see from their wallpaper just that the English are aiming for. This is wallpaper that is not ashamed to be made of paper. And why should it be? There are certain wall coverings that cost more, but the Englishman is not a parvenu. In his home, it could never occur to anyone that the money had run out.

Personal Interest

For those of you that haven't had the opportunity to meet all of us in person, here's your chance to put a face with a name. We asked everyone to march down to the local diner photo booth along with a prop, and give us a glimpse of themselves! We think the results are quite revealing. Please don't be shy, drop by and see us any time, or make plans to attend one of our art shows. We think of our clients, staff, partners, and friends as a family, come and get to know us!

Event Calendar

Maddocks & Company

Principals: Frank Maddocks, David Stern, Mary Scott, Curt Altmann, Sean Adams, Noreen Morioka.
Year Founded: 1975
Size of Firm: 40
Key Clients:
Bristol Meyers, Columbia Tristar Internaional Television, Coty-Lancaster, Joico Laboratories, The Limited, MGM-United Artists, Philips Media, Procter & Gamble, Showtime Netowrks, Sony Computer Entertainment, Walt Disney Comapny, Warner Bros.

2011 Pontius Avenue
Los Angeles, CA 90025
310.477.4227
www.maddocks.com

(at press time, Adams Morioka, Inc. had merged with Maddocks & Co.)

addocks & Company states this as its signature philosophy: There is no decorative "style" layered on top of a product; all work produced is based on a true effort to understand the client's needs and criteria; embracing a rigorous program of skill and high-quality production; providing unexpected but direct ideas; designing a solution that produces results. The firm has expanded to both coasts and has become a destination for clients interested in a full range of services: packaging systems to broadcast design; interactive and internet capabilities to environmental, signage and most recently—interiors. There is an energy at Maddocks & Company that pervades. The design department is built on the model of George Nelson at Herman Miller, a stable of one of the most talented designers in Los Angeles and New York. The designers collaboratively work together along with the client and account services department. All of the company's designers come from a wide range of backgrounds and produce surprising and diverse work. From the flurry of activity and experimentation, commiment to retaining high standards in every aspect of design, in-depth communication with the client, down to the final product—on the shelf, in the mail or via satellite—Maddocks & Company generates excitement and results.

above
Comprehensive package, identity and naming program for three lines of children's bath for Disney Consumer Products, Burbank, CA. The products—developed by Gryphon Development, New York, NY—strikes a balance between bath elements and character-driven graphics.

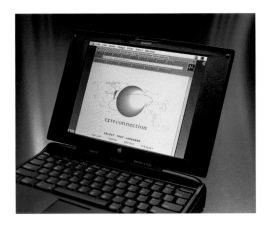

BookNet™

above from left to right
Frank Maddocks,
Mary Scott, David Stern,
Sean Adams,
Noreen Morioka.

left and right
Identity for Booknet, New
York, NY, a cable channel
that specializes in books and
authors. The solution combines the power of books,
the original mass medium,
with today's macro mass
medium—television.

The Fashion Institute
of Design & Merchandising

FIDM

left
Website for Fashion
Institute of Design and
Merchandising, Los Angeles,
CA. To provide FIDM with
an effective marketing vehicle that takes full advantage
of new technology, the site
gives the prospective students
24-hour informational access.
Key sections are divided by
mastheads and a consistent
editorial style, reflecting the
culture of the school and serving as an industry resource.

above
Identity, merchandising,
display, graphics and naming system for i.d., a line
of cosmetics for Bare
Escentuals, San Fransisco,
CA. Designed to work in
the Bare Escentuals store
environment, the program
expresses a young, under-
stated and sophisticated
sensibility.

opposite page bottom left
Comprehensive identity
program and Website
interface design for
CityConnection, New York,
NY—the first worldwide
virtual guide to major cities.
To succeed as the leading
online guide, it needed to be
easily accessible and visually
interesting, allowing for
multiple levels of search
categories and attracting
advertisers to support the site.

above and right
Collateral for a special fundraising event at The American Craft Museum, New York, NY. The promotional packet included an invitation, catalog, posters and t-shirts. Since the theme was the "American Banquet," tableware was combined with vintage photography of elegant banquets from the past. Archives were searched and staff members brought in photos of their own family banquets. The invitations were hand-folded like a napkin, and the paper stock gave the tactile sense of table linen.

right
Identity for Gelson's Markets, Los Angeles, CA. To leverage the image of the upscale supermarket into an unique identity for a spin-off retail concept—Gelson's Cookware Connection—the nature of the store needed to be clearly communicated through elements such as shopping bags, signage and uniforms. The simple design helps to define the store's boundaries with an adjacent full-service supermarket.

gelson's
cookware
connection

left
Identity and materials for Venice Public Library's volunteer group, Venice, CA. The contemporary monogram is reminiscent of bookplates while capturing the colorful energy and heritage of the Venice community. The system allows for playful use of letterforms that can apply to all collateral.

right
Logo for the California
Sesquicentennial helps
the state to celebrate its
first 150 years. A dynamic,
flowing symbol adds an
energetic, celebratory note
to the wordmark, which
incorporates a proprietary
visual pun.

cal1**50**rnia™
SESQUICENTENNIAL

left and right
Concept, wordmark and
identity for a bath and
body line, Pacifica Produce
Company, for Gryphon
Development, New York,
NY. As a private label for
Mervyn's California, the
line needed to fit with
rebranding efforts for the
store. Photography and a
proprietary naming system
communicates the ingredient
"story" for each product,
giving it a whimsical appeal
for a younger audience.

below
Brand identity, name,
components, advertising
and graphics program for
Zegarelli, an upscale hair
care line for Cosmetics USA,
Los Angeles, CA. Embossing
was used to enhance brand
recognition.

below
Identity, product naming, packaging and collateral for the Murad 365 line of therapeutic beauty products by Murad, El Segundo, CA. A simple aesthetic evokes the tranquil ambiance of an exclusive spa environment.

below right
Program syndication package for Columbia TriStar Entertainment, Culver City, CA. To inform Sony Television's new South American market about the current showcase of programs offered for distribution, translucent layers of information—via vellum overlays—offset the tediousness of copy-heavy translations.

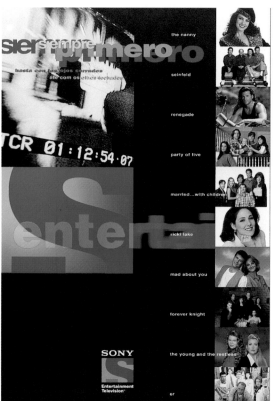

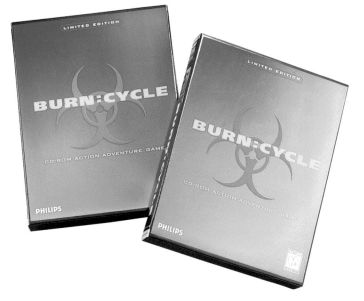

left
Package and collateral brochure for Burn: Cycle, Philips Interactive, Los Angeles, CA. Since the logotype developed for the game has a strong attitude, the design features it in a prominent and straightforward typographic style. Screened on a dispersed liquid-crystal substrate and fabricated into the package, it changes color when the consumer handles the package. Light temperature changes in the retail environment also continually affect its colors.

left, above and below
Brand identity, packaging systems, collateral and advertising design to launch the Sony Playstation, Sony Computer Entertainment, San Francisco, CA. The brand identity effectively communicates the power of the game player versus the competition.

below
Packaging system for Bell Sports, Los Gatos, CA. To provide the company with a dual packaging system that allows for the maintenance of brand equity while competing at diverse levels of distribution, mass market packaging emphasizes value and safety while Pro Series packaging communicates performance and sophistication. Both solved key design problems—while maintaining the Bell franchise name.

Maestri

Principal: Paula Rees
Year Founded: 1979
Size of Firm: 2 to ∞
Key Clients: Bank & Office
Interiors, Cineplex Odeon,
Emerald Downs, GATX,
Kepro, Prescott, Port of
Seattle, The Rouse
Company, Royal Caribbean
Cruise Lines, Seattle
Center, Sparling.

217 Pine Street
The Penthouse
Seattle, Washington 98101
206 622 4322

Maestri, meaning leaders in the arts, is also the name of a multi-disciplinary firm that assembles teams of collaborative experts for each project's specific requirements. The approach is the same—whether an intimate destination spa or civic project on an international scale. Art, theater, science and architecture are the backbone to the ideas and vision that supports Maestri's design. But it's serving the client rather than self-serving stardom that ultimately stimulates Maestri's "dream teams" and produces timeless solutions. "We're modern day alchemists," says Paula Rees, Maestri's principal. "Our clients provide us with different raw materials, and through a good process—and a little magic thrown in—we create gold."

above right
Information brochure for the Institute for Aesthetic Surgery in Kirkland, WA. The concept deals with the idea of "balance."
Designers, Paula Rees and Linda Soukup; copy, John Koval; photography, Ben Kerns.

below
Descriptive calligraphy created for Maestri.
Lettering, Greg Stadler.

above
A new urban myth created for the environmental graphics and renovation of the Seattle Center, the 1962 World's Fair site.
Design, Maestri and TRA Graphics; designers, Paula Rees, Jon Bentz and Linda Soukup; artist, Jeff Benesi; writer, Paula Rees.

Leaders in the Arts

left
From left: Paula Rees,
principal; Linda Soukup,
senior designer.

below
Announcement for the
5th Anniversary of Nakano
Dennis Landscape
Architects, Seattle, WA.
Five balanced rocks and
the pattern of native grasses
reflect the natural sensibility
of the firm.
Designers, Paula Rees and
Linda Soukup; photography,
Kevin LaTona.

*above, bottom right and
opposite page top*
Cast bronze sidewalk
plaques at City Centre in
Seattle, WA. The plaques
are outside all retail entries
to attract shoppers.
Designers, Paula Rees,
Bruce Hale and Greg
Stadler; copy, John Koval;
fabricator, SignTech.

left
Holiday wrapping paper for
employees of a Seattle coffee
franchise. Each paper has a
different pattern on the back.
Designers, Paula Rees, Linda
Soukup and Greg Stadler.

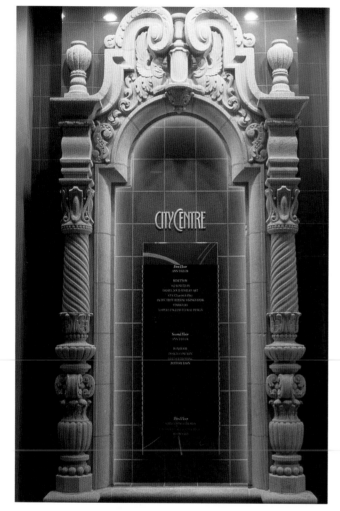

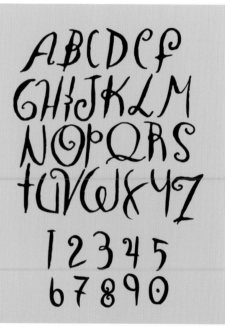

below
CD-ROM packaging and portfolio booklet for photographer Doug Plummer. Designers, Paula Rees and Linda Soukup.

below right
The brochure promotes Strathmore Paper Company's "Grandee" paper colors, while doubling as a capability piece for Maestri.

Design and copy, Paula Rees, John Koval and Linda Soukup.

above
Capabilities system for Sparling, Seattle, WA. To show the company's ability to connect new systems for cutting-edge technology companies, a series of primer books were created to humorously, but clearly, communicate a technically complex service. Design/Concept/Copy, Paula Rees, Linda Soukup and Greg Stadler.

above right
Business stationery for Maestri. The classic typography and symbols, used throughout the ages, have different esoteric meanings. Designers, Paula Rees and Linda Soukup; lettering, Ken Shafer.

above middle
Stationery design for Bruce MacDonald, Seattle, WA. As an architectural illustrator, the stationery features MacDonald's art on the back of various business cards, with a booklet-style envelope on complimentary stock. Designers, Paula Rees and Linda Soukup.

right
Client gift for Sparling Electrical Engineers, Seattle, WA. To acknowledge a client's 50th Anniversary, four limited-edition prints were produced of architectural paintings and overlayed with vellum for congratulatory text. Designers, Paula Rees and Linda Soukup; paintings, Richard Morhous.

below and right
Environmental graphics and marketing, including directory design and exterior signage at Northtown Mall, Spokane, WA. The retail directory is topped with custom glass fixtures by regional artists.
Designers, Paula Rees, Jeff Thompson, David Hoffman, Phil Jones and Greg Stadler; fabricator, SignTech.

right
Identity for Waterleaf Architects, Seattle, WA. The announcement and notecard are part of its new name, logotype, business papers, presentation systems and forms.
Designers, Paula Rees and Linda Soukup.

far right
Capability brochure for Potter & Associates, Seattle, WA. The project was meant to challenge the pressman on its new 5-color press, and show off its printing capabilities. The brochure worked immediately—bringing in one of the company's largest orders in 40 years.
Designers, Paula Rees and Linda Soukup; illustrator, Wendy Wortsman, Rep Art.

right
Environmental graphics for
Oxmoor Center, Louisville,
KY. The food court signage
is just one component of the
extensive renovation.
Designers, Paula Rees, Jeff
Thompson and David
Hoffman; illustrator, Jack
Molloy; fabricator, SignTech.

above and left
Prototypes of t-shirts and
cabin corridor signs for Royal
Caribbean Cruise Lines,
Miami, FL. Maestri was
involved in developing the
names for new megaships, as
well as the identity for all
the shops, restaurants, and
major public areas.
Collaborative team of
designers: Maestri,
TeamDesign, Kathy
Wesselman and John Koval.

top
Identity for Emerald Downs,
Auburn, WA, a new thor-
oughbred horse racing track.
The project included naming,
identity and environmental
graphics in collaboration
with TRA Graphics.
Designers, Paula Rees, Jon
Bentz, Linda Soukup, Scott
Souchock and Ken Shafer.

above
Stationery and packaging for
Spa Csaba, Kirkland, WA.
The project included logo-
type, packaging, environmen-
tal graphics and marketing
for a new waterfront spa.
Designers, Paula Rees, Linda
Soukup and Ken Shafer.

Marc English

Principal:
Marc English
Year Founded: 1993
Size of Firm: 1+
Key Clients: Boston
Film/Video Foundation,
Cambridge Friends School,
DOT05 Optical
Communications, Inc;
Fusion, Inc.; Hearst
Corporation, Houghton
Mifflin Publishing, Co.;
Marywood Children &
Family Services, Meta
Software Corporation,
Packaged Goods, Inc.; Sara
Lee Corporation, Texas
Fine Arts Association.

2414A South Lamar Blvd.
Austin, TX 78704
512 441 7215

■ ■ ■ arc English's visual language is best described as eclectic: Equally comfortable with clients of commerce or culture, his design vocabulary is steeped in history & story; Modernism & vernacular; precision & punk. The former Bostonian balances each while working with a variety of clients, infusing corporate work with spirit and *pro bono* work with marketing savvy. A writer once stated, "What makes English's work so successful is that he has managed to harness the tongue-in-cheek humor of postmodernism while omitting the clutter and smugness too often found in contemporary design." English's studies documenting Native American petroglyphs led to an understanding of visual communications that have stood the test of time and the realization that contemporary is often just temporary; that meaning gets lost. While counseling his students to use wit, insight and responsibility, in the end he advises of each project to "let it be what it wants to be."

left
Exhibition overview for
the Photographic Resource
Center, Boston, MA.
Art Director/Designer,
Marc English.

above
Poster for the Boston
Film/Video Foundation;
"An Evening With Laurie
Anderson" is a benefit by
the performance artist.
Art Director/Designer/
Typographer, Marc English.

left
At home on the range, the city and anywhere in between, design shaman Marc English humps his "John Henry"-model t-square from the wrong side of the tracks of the Missouri Pacific rail line in Texas.

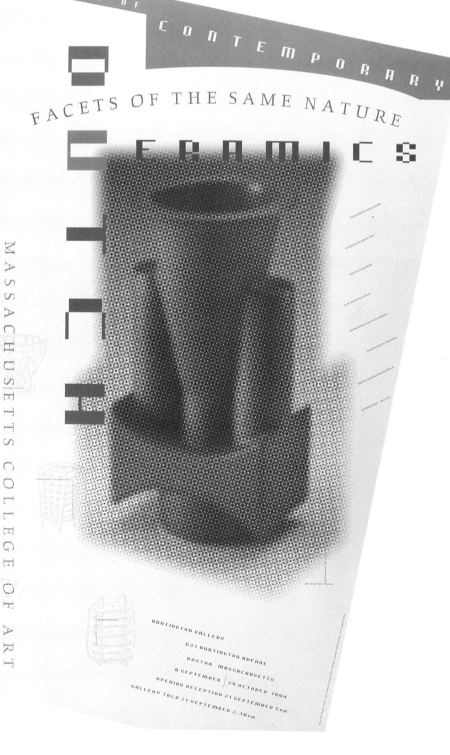

above
The three circles of the Medici crest—the pawn symbol—combined with native American art and 19th-century type to create a logo for Buffalo Pawn, Dallas, TX.
Art Director/Designer, Marc English.

right
Poster for Massachusetts College of Art, "Facets of the Same Nature: A Survey of Contemporary Dutch Ceramics."
Art Director, Marc English; designers, English and Chris Goviea; photography, Pieter Vandermeer; illustrator, Lans Stroeve.

right
Poster for "Touch of Power:
Media for a New Age,"
lectures, AIGA/Boston.
Art Director/Designer/
Photography, Marc English.

below
Identity for Boston Brownies,
based in the historic Faneuil
Hall Marketplace of Boston.
Art Director/Designer,
Marc English.

bottom
Visions, a quarterly journal
for the Boston Film/Video
Foundation.
Art Director/Designer,
Marc English.

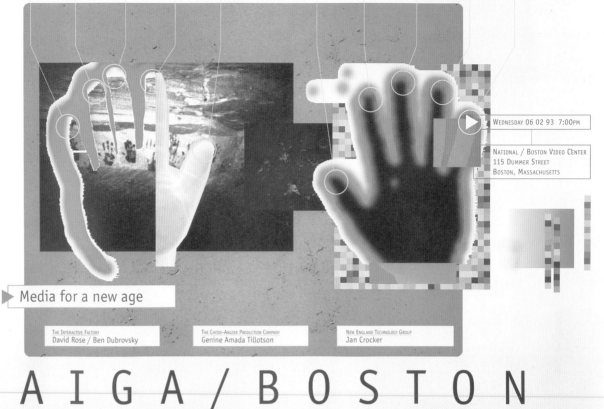

T O U C H OF P O W E R

Media for a new age

WEDNESDAY 06 02 93 7:00PM

NATIONAL / BOSTON VIDEO CENTER
115 DUMMER STREET
BOSTON, MASSACHUSETTS

THE INTERACTIVE FACTORY
David Rose / Ben Dubrovsky

THE CHEDD-ANGIER PRODUCTION COMPANY
Genine Amada Tillotson

NEW ENGLAND TECHNOLOGY GROUP
Jan Crocker

A I G A / B O S T O N

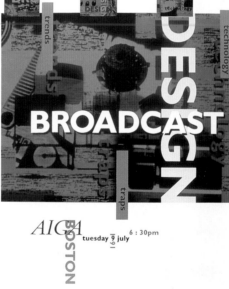

above
Poster for "Broadcast
Design: Trends, Traps and
Technology," AIGA/Boston.
Art Director, Marc English;
designers, English and
Tom Nielsen.

right
Book jacket for *The Ville:
Cops & Kids in Urban
America*, Houghton Mifflin,
Co., Boston, MA.
Art Director, Michaela
Sullivan; designer,
Marc English.

below
"(Cult)ivate Culture:
*La Sirena, El Musico, El
Mundo, La Muerte*" a visual
story told with Mexican
loteria cards, serve as self-
promotional poster series.
Art Director/Designer,
Marc English.

right
Identity for Massachusetts
Association of Bank
Counsel, Boston.
Art Director, Marc English;
designers, English and
Ash Pigford.

BLiNDeD
BY
THe LiGHt
?

above
Logo for television
special on religious cults,
WCVB TV, Needham, MA.
Art Director/Designer,
Marc English.

left
Invitation and program for
"Distinguished Citizen
Award Dinner." It plays off
1940s Scout manual for
Middlesex Council, Boy
Scouts of America.
Art Director/Designer,
Marc English.

right
Book cover for About
Language, Houghton
Mifflin, Co. Neo-cuneiform,
contemporary stencils and
word shapes serve as visual
interest for this college
textbook.
Art Director, Anthony
Saizon; designer,
Marc English.

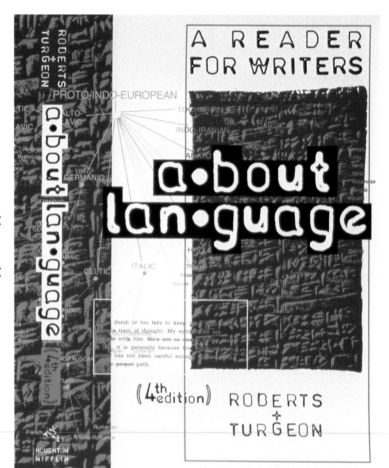

above
Logo for Xygraphix
Corporation, Boston, MA.
Art Director/Designer,
Marc English.

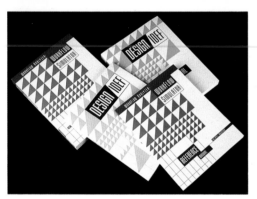

top
Capabilities brochure,
direct marketing brochure
and software manual
design for Meta Software,
Cambridge, MA.
Art Director/Designer,
Marc English.

above
Software manual design
for Meta Software. Although
these patterns are used in
a variety of contexts around
the world, here they provide
a virtual diagram of the
client's software application.
Art Director/Designer,
Marc English.

right
Walter Compton
Retrospective exhibition
catalog for Massachusetts
College of Art.
Art Director, Marc English;
designers, English, Jake
Hooten and Ash Pigford.

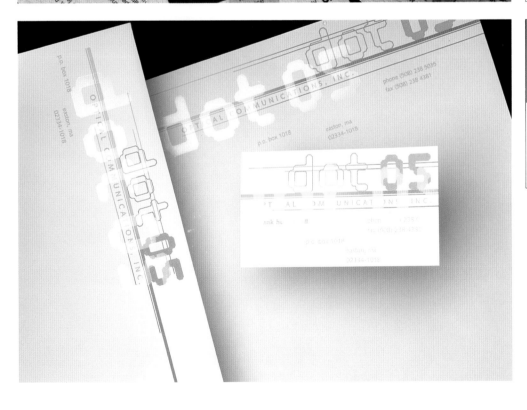

left
Cards for AIGA/Boston. "On Deck: '94-'95 Season Board of Directors" provide vital statistics and mission statements for AIGA/Boston. Art Director/Designer, Marc English; illustrators, James Kraus and Ben Franklin.

below
Cover for *Recreational Facilities Design*, highlighting the Pyramid Arena in Memphis, for Rockport Publishers, Rockport, MA. Art Director, Laura Herrmann; designer, Marc English.

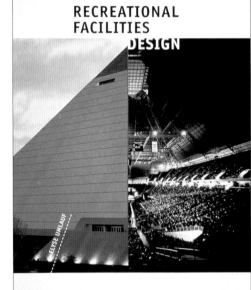

above
Book jackets for Houghton Mifflin, Co. Art Director, Michaela Sullivan; designer, Marc English.

left
Identity for DOT 05 Optical Communications, Inc., Norwood, MA, is conveyed with metallic and florescent inks and transparent foil stamp. Art Director, Marc English; designers, English and Jake Hooten.

May & Co.

Principal: Douglas May
Date Founded: 1985
Size of Firm: 5
Key Clients:
Aetna, AmFAR, AudioNet,
Blue Cross Blue Shield of
Texas, CNET, Inc., eAuto,
Homart, Lincoln Property
Company, Memorex Telex,
Neiman Marcus, Overhead
Door Corp., PageNet,
Papertech, PC ServiceSource,
Texas Instruments, Units,
The Washington Opera

5401 N. Central Expwy.
Suite 325
Dallas, TX 75205
214 528 4770
www.mayandco.com

May & Co. was founded on the precept that ideas are the foundation for design; the fuel for creativity. Together with sound strategic planning, this can be a formidable communication force, whatever the medium. Putting this ideology into practice is Douglas May, a 1980 graduate of the Art Center College of Design in Pasadena, California who began his professional career in New York, working as Art Director for media guru Roger Black and designer for type genius Tom Carnase. Returning to his native Dallas under the employ of Stan Richards, Doug later formed May & Co., now in its twelfth year of operation. The firm provides cross media solutions ranging from corporate communications and identity management to product packaging, web site and multimedia design. This approach has won not only the patronage of a national base of clients, but also the recognition of the New York Directors Club, Communication Arts, American Institute of Graphic Arts, Print, Type Directors Club, and Graphis to name but a few.

top
Theme catalogue created for Neiman Marcus, Dallas, TX. The design features high-end incentives and corporate gifts from this internationally respected retailer under the banner of 'measuring success'.

left
Brand development and packaging system for Altsys, Richardson, TX. Virtuoso is a Unix based design, drawing and production software program.

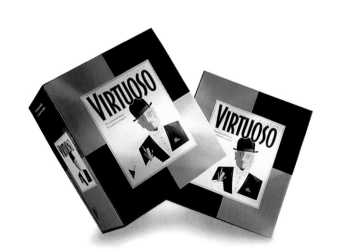

right
Brochure for computer parts
distributor PC Service
Source. This presentation
folder doubles as a corporate
capabilities brochure that
was written and designed
to position the company for
rapid domestic and international growth. The company
specializes in after-market
replacement parts for
over 29 original equipment
manufactures.

right
May & Co. developed the
retail image and support
collateral for Units,
Garland, TX; a women's
fashion manufacturer
and division of JCPenny.

::units®

opposite page and above
Series of internal newslet-
ters for PageNet, Plano, TX.
This organization maintains
a very segmented employee
base in offices across the
continent. The format had
to appeal to their youthful
age bracket and instill a
sense of comradeship
between regional offices.

right
Concert invitation head-
lining musician Paul Simon;
the event was a benefit
for AmFAR, the American
Foundation for AIDS
Research, Los Angeles, CA.

right
Architectural design manual for Overhead Door Corporation, Dallas, TX. Manufactured from its product materials, this manual includes exhaustive descriptions of its entire manufacturing line: product listings, elevations, isometric and exploded views by category. The manual is targeted to architects needing easy access to drawings and specifications that they can, in turn, utilize for plans.

bottom and opposite page
Interactive architectural design manual for Overhead Door Corporation; an outgrowth of the printed collateral, utilizing the same organizational hierarchy. The proposed CD-ROM application allows architects to view products in full 3-D animation and download electronic product files for use in CAD plotting and blueprinting.

below
Naming and online branding for electronic banking software that allows corporate CFO's secured transactions via proprietary technology. Created for TeamBank, Dallas, TX.

above

Annual report for PageNet, Dallas, TX. Individual customers were profiled for using their services in interesting ways. This spread features a hydroponic lettuce farmer who monitors and regulates the environment in his greenhouse via remote with an alpha-numeric pager.

right

Capabilities brochure for Restaurant Services Inc., Dallas, TX, an institutional restaurant fixture fabricator; they design, manufacture and install restaurant equipment worldwide.

far right

Home page design for eAuto, Dallas, TX, an internet site that provides access to everything automotive and other web pages relating to the automotive industry. Visit the entire site at www.eauto.com.

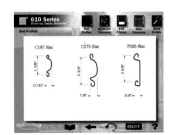

right, clockwise
World premier promotional poster announcing performances of 'The Dream of Valentino' for The Washington Opera at Kennedy Center, Washington, D.C. Poster announcing a lecture by Tomatsu Yagi, Esprit designer, for the Dallas Society of Visual Communications. Promotional poster for Heritage Press, Dallas, TX; comparing quotes from Eric Gill's 'Essay on Typography' circa 1936, and Nicholas Negroponte's 'Being Digital' circa 1995, which communicate similar positions on technology vs. quality.

below, left to right
Logos for Audionet, Dallas, TX; Imagination Incorporated, Chicago IL; Intex Software, Las Colinas, TX; The Washington Opera, Washington, D.C.; Type 94, San Francisco, CA; Third Rock Technology, Pittsburgh, PA; PageNet, Plano, TX; Martin Sinkoff Wines, Inc., Dallas, TX.

bottom, left to right
Season promotional poster for The Washington Opera at Kennedy Center. Poster announcing the Seventh Annual Dallas Designer's Chili Cookoff. Cover for annual Best & Worst issue of D Magazine the city magazine of Dallas, TX.

right
Promotional program for
Papertech, a division of
Classen Papier KG, Stuttgart,
Germany. In addition to
introducing new corporate
identity, the 'Papertech
Paper Reference System'
includes swatchbooks, grade
comparisons, pricing information, terms and stocking
information; everything
their customers need to specify paper in a vehicle that
is easy to access and update.

left
Worldwide packaging for
Texas Instruments con-
sumer electronics, Dallas,
TX. The arched top was a
new approach to a very traditional packaging method
differentiating TI products
from their competitors,
while maintaining consis-
tency throughout the various lines with clear links to
their corporate identity.

left
Little Black Book member-
ship directory for the Dallas
Society of Visual Communications. Now in its sixth
edition, this listing is very
popular among club members
because it is small, easy to
reference, and easily updated.

Mires Design Inc.

Principals: Scott Mires,
José Serrano, John Ball
Year Founded: 1983
Size of Firm: 11
Key Clients: AirTouch
Cellular, Boyd Coffee,
California Center for the
Arts, Compton's New
Media, Deleo Clay Tile,
FoundStuff Paperworks,
Harcourt Brace & Co., Intel,
Nike, Taylor Guitars,
The National Basketball
Association, Voit Sports, Inc.

2345 Kettner Boulevard
San Diego, CA 92101
619 234 6631
www.miresdesign.com

Mires Design has grown steadily on the strength of its reputation for strategic thinking and creative excellence. Since its founding in 1983, the firm has used a benefit-oriented approach to solve communication problems, build brand identities and generate results. This means working closely with clients to refine the message. It means the visuals and words work together to support the message. And it can mean foregoing the fashionable in favor of more appropriate and enduring solutions. Mires Design's idea-based work has earned national recognition, as well as rewarding relationships with clients from coast to coast.

above
Packaging design for
FoundStuff Paperworks,
San Diego, CA. Made out
of 100 percent recycled
chipboard and post-consumer
waste, the design reflects
old-world imagery while
effectively communicating
within the modern retail
environment.
Art Director/Designer,
José Serrano; illustrator,
Tracy Sabin; production,
Miguel Perez.

left
Identity program for a music
production house, Ear to
Ear, Los Angeles, CA.
Because the company creates
jingles, soundtracks and
original scores, upbeat
graphics and whimsical
designs were used to visually
depict an aural experience.
Art Directors, Scott Mires
and José Serrano;
designers, Mires and
Deborah Fukushima;
illustrator, Tracy Sabin.

right
Left to right: Eric Freedman, John Ball, Deborah Hom, Miguel Perez, Scott Mires, Anne Brower, Kathy Carpentier-Moore, José Serrano, Toni MacCabe, Daisy Fukushima and Mike Brower.

Truck series design for the *San Diego Union-Tribune*, San Diego, CA. The paper was getting a new fleet of delivery trucks and wanted to apply more interesting graphics than the paper's name. The idea of the paper's "moving billboard" was born. "Our solutions were interesting to look at with a subtle newspaper reference, which received a lot of attention from people on the road."
Art Director/Designer, José Serrano.

below
The "People Reading" truck shows the diversity of the paper's audience.
Photography, Chris Wimpey.

bottom right
The cat/dog chase was a humorous answer to this truck. On one side the dog is chasing the cat, the other side the cat is chasing the dog, and on the back both sit side-by-side.
Illustrator, Braldt Bralds.

left
An integral part of the Sunday paper—the funnies. Different truck-trailer comics include: Beetle Bailey, shown, (illustrator, Mort Walker), Blondie (illustrators, Dean Young and Stan Drake), and Rex Morgan, M.D. (illustrators, Woody Wilson and Tony DiPreta).

above
Point of purchase display for Deleo Clay Tile Co., Lake Elsinore, CA. To introduce a new line of European-style roofing tiles, old-world charm and quality craftsmanship were blended to create a new but classical look.
Art Director, José Serrano; designers, Serrano, Miguel Perez; photography, Carl VanderSchuit.

below
Promotional calendar given to Deleo customers, architects and roofers. It intertwines a theme about a year in the life of a roofer with the company's products.
Art Director, José Serrano; designers, Serrano and Miguel Perez; copywriter, Kelly Smothermon.

right
Identity package that includes a yard sign, a placard and a binder containing price lists, brochures and specs for the roofing tiles. Designer, José Serrano; illustrator, Nancy Stahl.

below right
Boxes to ship samples to customers. The design conveys the natural qualities of the clay tiles inside.
Art Director/Designer, José Serrano; illustrator, Tracy Sabin.

Just can't leave those computer engineering challenges at the office? This story is for you.

"It's amazing how far into the future a 4-mile run can take you."

{ Advancing optical storage systems meant taking exactly the right steps.

Needless to say, this is not your typical bedtime story.

"What we really wanted to roll out was a breakthrough technology."

{ Developing an advanced network intelligent wiring hub takes just the right kind of equipment.

A convincing argument that computer engineering could be at least as exciting as anything in sports, if only ESPN would cover it.

"I'm really not sure where the tennis game stopped and the problem-solving started."

{ Some initial work on the 5-channel EISA disk array controller.

Smaller, Lighter and Smarter.

To Make Products

A New Way

Introducing

above
Direct-mail testimonial campaign for Intel Corporation, Santa Clara, CA. Real interviews brought a human and often humorous twist to successful product design. Stories were used to entice engineers to specify the i960 processor in their own projects.
Art Director, Scott Mires; designers, Mires and Deborah Fukushima; photography, Marshall Harrington.

left
Intel's 1994 annual report, also produced for the World Wide Web, uses a mix of photography and illustration to communicate the company's message and presence in the consumer PC marketplace.
Art Director, John Ball; designers, Ball, Kathy Carpentier-Moore and Miguel Perez; editor, Sandra Rosenzweig.

left
The boxes progressively decreasing in size shows that SmartDie, a new Intel product, can help make products smaller, lighter and smarter.
Art Director/Designer, Scott Mires.

Exhibition materials for California Center for the Arts, Escondido, CA.

right
Catalog for an exhibition of animal-inspired artwork. A look was created for the exhibition that could be merchandised on T-shirts, mugs, banners, etc., without detracting from the exhibit itself.
Art Director, John Ball; designers, Ball, and Gale Spitzley.

bottom left
Catalog for an exhibition of big, bright, contemporary California sculpture. The artist's essays are designed to reflect their artwork, while the yellow paper stock keeps them visually separate from the coated artwork pages.
Art Director, John Ball; designers, Ball and Deborah Fukushima.
bottom right
Quarterly newsletter that informs members about various events offered at this center for performing and visual arts.
Art Directors, John Ball and José Serrano; designers, Ball and Miguel Perez; photography, Carl VanderSchuit.

left
"The Orb" basketballs for Voit Sports, Inc., Carlsbad, CA. The new line has a unique grip that allows youths to palm the ball. The hand graphic helps to illustrate this feature. Art Director, José Serrano; designers, Michael Brower and Serrano; illustrator, Tracy Sabin.

below
Poster for the San Diego Antique Motorcycle Club. The poster captures the history and drama of motorcycle racing with vivid photography. Art Director, John Ball; designers, Ball and Miguel Perez; photography, Chris Wimpey.

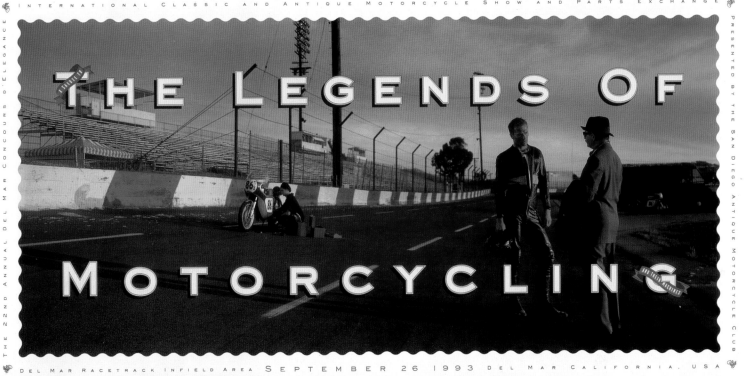

far left
Point-of-purchase display for LA Gear, Santa Monica, CA. The illuminated display helps reinforce the nature of the product by using light cartridges and batteries that are used in its illuminated footwear. Art Director/Designer, Scott Mires; illustrator, Tracy Sabin.

left
Publication for Ektelon, San Diego, CA. To introduce its new line of racquetball products, a brochure and magazine were blended into one publication. Art Director, José Serrano; designers, Michael Brower and Serrano; photography, Carl VanderSchuit.

Modern Dog
Commercial Art

Principals: Robynne Raye, Michael Strassburger
Year Founded: 1987
Size of Firm: 5
Key Clients: A&M Records, Capitol Records, Rhino Records, Warner Bros. Records, Experience Music Project, Fremont Fair, Seattle Repertory Theatre, Nissan, Showtime, Nike, K2 Snowboards, Northwest AIDS Foundation.

7903 Greenwood Avenue N
Seattle, WA 98103
206 789 POOP

 odern Dog? Here's the idea: come up with colorful, funny, provocative, in-your-face, on-the-money, can't-ignore-it, hocus-pocus answers to the same old questions. Do it for bigwigs like Nike or Showtime. Do it for the art gallery that's opening two blocks down, or for the Northwest AIDS Foundation. Do it for your cousin Joe—it doesn't matter! What does matter is that you're having a great time; you spend your days in a big funky house, surrounded by music, toys, a scrappy Westie, a skinny Whippet, a big ol' grumpy mutt and work samples from your favorite jobs—theatre posters, television commercials, snowboards, Japanese skis, magazine ads, Internet pages, wedding invitations—whatever! To you, they all represent the same thing; a whole lotta fun. And that's what Modern Dog is all about. Everything else? Pure gravy.

left and below
Fur box portfolio. The custom synthetic fur box is complete with a studded collar and engraved name tag, and always stocked with samples and free treats. Art Directors, Robynne Raye and Michael Strassburger; designers, Raye, Strassburger and Vittorio Costarella.

left
Self-promotional, limited edition, hand-numbered deck of 52 playing cards, each displaying a different Modern Dog piece. Art Directors, Robynne Raye and Michael Strassburger; package designer, Strassburger; Joker designers, Vittorio Costarella and George Estrada.

opposite page right
Collectible, screen-printed paper samples for a new line of colors by Gilbert Paper, Menasha, WI. The illustrations helped to highlight 10 new paper colors by only screen-printing in black and white.
Creative Director, Sharon Chandler; art director, Michael Strassburger; designers/illustrators/copywriters, Strassburger, Robynne Raye, Vittorio Costarella and George Estrada; copywriter, Anna McAllister.

left
Left to right: George Estrada,
Robynne Raye, Michael
Strassburger, Coby Schultz
and Vittorio Costarella.
Photography,
Savey Security Systems.

right
Holiday Favorites cookbook
and mailer for Warner Bros.
Records, Burbank, CA. All
recipes are submitted by
recording artists. The book's
copywriters?... Eddie Van
Halen, Johnny Cash, Joan
Jett, Madonna and others.
Art Director, Jeri Heiden;
designer/illustrator,
Vittorio Costarella.

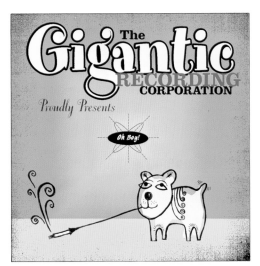

above
Left to right: CD covers
of Alternative Sampler for
Giant Records, Beverly
Hills, CA.
Designer/Illustrator,
Robynne Raye.
Music convention sampler
for A&M Records,
Hollywood, CA.
Art Director, Jeri Heiden,
designer/illustrator,
Michael Strassburger.
Anthology of the Kingston
Trio while on Capitol
Records, Hollywood, CA.
Art Directors, Jeff Fey and
Tommy Steele;
designer/illustrator,
Vittorio Costarella.

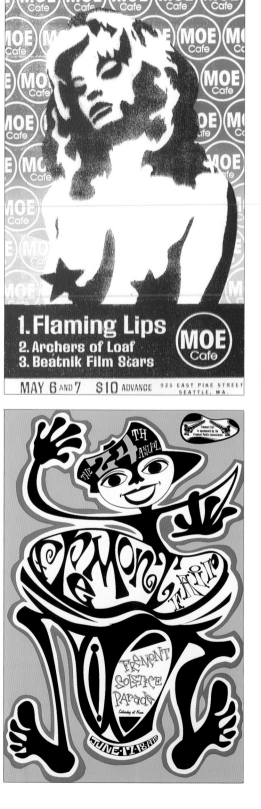

below/top row
Poster of the play *Heartbreak House* for the Seattle Reperatory Theatre, Seattle, WA. Designer/Illustrator, Vittorio Costarella.

Poster of the Jimi Hendrix Museum Rock Arena, for the Experience Music Project, Bellevue, WA. The museum sponsored a rock stage at Seattle's annual arts and music festival. Designer/Illustrator, Michael Strassburger.

Poster for One Reel, Seattle, WA. Bumbershoot is the city's annual urban arts and music festival. Designer/Illustrator, Robynne Raye.

below/bottom row
Poster of a live performance at ACT Theatre, Seattle, WA. *Man of the Moment* is a story about media exploitation. Designers, Robynne Raye and Michael Strassburger; illustrator, Raye.

Poster design for ACT Theatre, Seattle, WA. The play is about a logger that meets up with a Yeti and struggles with deforestation. Designer/Illustrator, Michael Strassburger.

Poster for Rainy States Film Festival, Seattle, WA, an annual festival that features independent filmmakers from the Pacific Northwest. Designer/Illustrator, Vittorio Costarella.

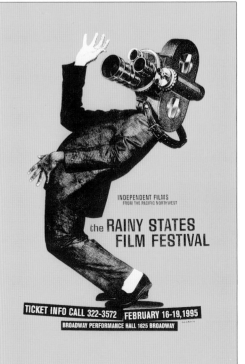

above
Characters for K2 Japan, Tokyo. (Boomerang Boy, Scorcher, Killer Bee, Scorpion, Mamba and B. Girl). Applications include skis, trade show booths, comic books, T-shirts, and other paraphernalia. Inventors/Illustrators, Vittorio Costarella, George Estrada and Michael Strassburger.

below
Brochures for K2 Snowboards, Vashon, WA. The images are inspired by the

Sears 1972 Spring catalog. Art Director, Michael Strassburger; designers/illustrators, Strassburger, Vittorio Costarella and George Estrada.

bottom
Consumer brochure of K2 Snowboards. No budget='zine look. Art Directors, Brent, Luke and Hayley; designers/illustrators,

Vittorio Costarella, Michael Strassburger, George Estrada and Robynne Raye.

right
QI Snowboards, a specialty line for K2, Vashon, WA. The El Limbo and Squid are two of the four QI boards. Designer/Illustrator for El Limbo, Vittorio Costarella; designer/illustrator for Squid, George Estrada.

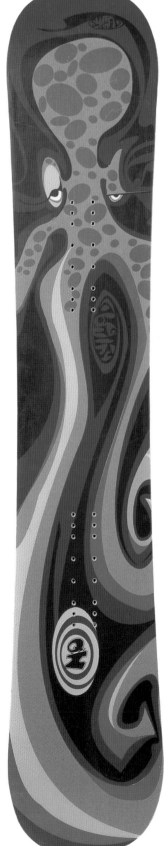

Partners Design, Inc.

Principals:
Jack Gernsheimer,
Jeff Gernsheimer
Year Founded: 1971
Size of Firm: 7
Key Clients: Armstrong
World Industries, Arrow
International, AT&T,
Black & Decker, Campbell's
Soup, Colgate/Palmolive,
Dana Corporation, Sweet
Street Desserts, Thonet
Industries, University of
Pennsylvania, World
Environment Center,
Zeneca Pharmaceuticals.

187 Koenig Road
Bernville, PA 19506
610 488 7611
www.partnerspa.com

Partners Design enjoys a relationship between principals Jack and Jeff Gernsheimer that began long before their alliance as business partners. Identical twins, the brothers attribute much of their success to their exceptional closeness. Together they have achieved far more than they could have alone. Traveling along a country road in Bernville, Pennsylvania will take you to the 200-year-old farmhouse that has been the firm's home for the last 25 years. Behind the idyllic exterior is a productive community of designers who provide honest solutions for clients ranging from AT&T to the local florist. Regardless of a job's size, Partners Design consistently strives to provide more than their clients expect, raise local design standards, and maintain a balance between personal interests and professional challenges. The company's staff—currently at seven (including another set of identical twins)—has remained small throughout the years. However, its range of endeavors continues to grow, now including identity programs, brochures and collateral materials; annual reports, packaging, advertising, environmental graphics, and most recently, internet-oriented design.

above and left
Brochure for a newly manufactured line of furniture classics, Thonet Industries, Statesville, NC. Designed to depict the product's craftsmanship and convey a sense of the classical foundations of the company, the photographs, while having an archival, classical quality, are framed by rough, impressionistic borders, suggesting the modern appeal of the furniture. The combination of classical and modern aesthetics are reinforced by showing Thonet's period logos throughout the pages. Designer, Jack Gernsheimer; photography, Steve Cicero.

left
Four-year-old Jack and Jeff Gernsheimer.
Photography, Dad.

right
Logos for The Neversink Brewing Company and The Canal Street Pub and Restaurant, Reading, PA. Known as a major beer-producing city, (John Updike dubbed it "Brewer" in his *Rabbit* series), Neversink is Reading's first new brewery since the prohibition. The logo evokes tradition and history. The Canal Street logo visually compliments the brewery, which coexists in a renovated factory building. Designer, Jack Gernsheimer.

left
Patterned fabric designed for Graco Children's Products, Inc., Elverson, PA. Studies have suggested that infants are stimulated by the black and white shapes. The fabric shows various animal forms without using literal illustrations. Using primary spot coloring makes the animal's eyes stand out for contrast. Designer, Jack Gernsheimer.

Brochure and other collateral for Sweet Street Desserts, Reading, PA. As the leading national manufacturer and distributor of gourmet desserts, the visual identity needed to appeal to both the wholesale food service industry and individual buyers. To further enhance the product's appeal, highly-stylized,

whimsical photography coupled with a running storyline was used to entertain customers.
Art Director, Sandy Solmon; designer, Jack Gernsheimer; photography, Nora Scarlett; set painting, Joy Nagy.

above
Corporate logo for an international importer of fresh produce, GreenStripe Inc., Philadelphia, PA. Considering research obtained through a collaboration with Crossroads Studios, the design needed to reflect the company's organic products and its continuing expansion.
Art Director, Dennis Brubaker; designer, Jack Gernsheimer.

left
An extensive line of literature for Arrow International, Inc., Reading, PA. The company manufactures critical-care and interventional medical devices used to diagnose and treat critically ill patients. Bright colors and variable rectangular grids bring energy and flexibility to the literature without compromising the seriousness of the subject.
Art Directors, Jeff Gernsheimer and Rick Yanchuleff; designer, Jennifer Hanf; photography; Steve Cicero and Doug Nicotera.

right
Stationery for Bryn Heist, Registered Architect, Reading, PA. The Registered Architect Seal combined with elements borrowed from blueprints effectively conveys the client's occupation as an independent architect. The colors and flexible scaling of the seal relate to the client's personable, accessible nature.
Designer, Jack Gernsheimer.

left
Logo for National Food Products, Ltd., Reading, PA. Although NFP specializes in the growth and distribution of mushrooms, one of the primary objectives was to address the company's anticipation of national expansion into other areas of the food service industry. Fusing the initials N and F, the evolution of the blue, banner-like arms into green leaves with a star in the middle represents its "National" interests. Designer, Jack Gernsheimer.

below
Logo design for the Holocaust Library at Albright College, Reading Jewish Federation, Reading, PA. The intersection of the pages of six opened books form the Star of David. The convergence of the lines conveys the intensity of the subject. Designer, Jack Gernsheimer.

The Holocaust Library and Resource Center at Albright College

Established by The Jewish Federation of Reading

In memory of those who

above
Visual identity program for Commercial Design & Furnishings, Inc., Reading PA. The CD&F logo is used with large graphic elements and scales. The letterhead and folder are die-cut with a serrated edge, reinforcing the fabric-swatch theme established in the logo. Designer, Jack Gernsheimer.

below
Identity program for a multi-faceted land development program, Spring Ridge, Inc., Wyomissing, PA. Bright colors and abstract images were used throughout the program. Applications included stationery, literature, advertising and signage. Art Director, Jeff Gernsheimer; designer, Jennifer Hanf; logo design, Jack Gernsheimer and Jeff Gernsheimer.

left
Direct mail campaign
promoting different ser-
vices offered by Entech
Engineering, Inc., Reading,
PA. Each of the four mailers in the series deals with
a different aspect of the
company's corporate strategy.
Received in a sequence,
potential clients were not
overloaded with a lot of
information all at once.
Art Director, Jeff
Gernsheimer; designer,
Jennifer Hanf.

above
Annual report cover of a
specialty steel manufacturer,
Carpenter Technology
Corporation, Reading, PA.
In 1993 the company suc-
ceeded in building their
100- plus year-old core business, expanding its global
interests and developing
new product lines. The single, non-traditional image
on the cover reflects these
achievements.
Art Director, Jack
Gernsheimer; designer,
Jennifer Hanf.

below right
Capabilities brochure for
Dana Corporation, Spicer
Systems Assembly Division,
Wyomissing, PA; with ex-
tended applications to envi-
ronmental graphics for the
company's corporate head-
quarters and plants in South
Carolina and Pennsylvania.
The photographs and graph-
ics used in the original
brochure became the basic
components of the interior
designs applied in various
areas of the company.
Art Director, Jeff
Gernsheimer; designers,
Jeff Gernsheimer and
Jason Wister; photography,
Theodore Anderson.

far right
Main entrance of Dana
Spicer's truck chassis
assembly plant, Lugoff, SC.
Brushed aluminum chassis
carries the graphic theme
established in the company's
capabilities brochure.
Designer, Jeff Gernsheimer;
production, L&H Signs.

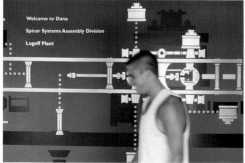

left
Packaging design for Clover Farms, Reading, PA, a regional producer of dairy products and other beverages. Analysis by CrossRoads Studio provided a design strategy for the entire line of products.
Art Director, Dennis Brubaker; designers, Jack Gernsheimer and Jeff Gernsheimer.

above
Logo for Philly Fresh, Philadelphia, PA, a small food distributor with plans to expand. The visual pun linking "Philly" with the image of a sprinting horse reflects the spirit of the company.
Art Director, Dennis Brubaker; designer, Jack Gernsheimer.

above
Capabilities brochure for Herbein+Company, Inc., Reading, PA, a medium-sized accounting firm that markets primarily to the dairy industry. Illustrations conveyed the company's friendly atmosphere, substi-tuting the traditional photography often utilized in depicting accounting firms. Incorporating a hint of the financial grid used on ledger sheets served as a consistent, but subtle background motif.
Designer, Jeff Gernsheimer; illustrator, Bruno Paciulli.

right
Identity program for Berks Packing Company, Reading, PA. The logo, seen on the left field wall of Reading Municipal Stadium, is used on stationery, signage, vehicles, uniforms and packaging for a variety of meat products such as hot dogs, bacon and hams.
Designer, Jack Gernsheimer; calligraphy, Jim Lebbad.

post tool

Principal: Gigi Biederman,
David Karam
Year Founded: 1993
Size of Firm: 2
Key Clients: Bay Area
Playwrights, California
College of Arts and Crafts,
Colossal Pictures, Four Walls,
frogdesign, Lunar, Organic
Online, Schlumberger,
Sprint Telecommunication,
Steelcase, Swatch,
Time/Warner Cable,
Warner Records.

301 Eighth Street
Suite 230
San Francisco, CA 94103
415 255 1094

 ost tool design comes from the meeting of two extremes—fine art melded with technology. Using a menagerie of elements, the firm has created a vocabulary spanning into print, interactive design, video, animation and installation. Gigi Biederman and David Karam design by free association, inspired by iconic imagery from high-and-low culture. post tool's projects have included photo collage and illustration, identity and website development, video production, installations and interactive kiosks.

opposite page/bottom
Interactive portfolio for
8, Inc., San Francisco, CA.
As a small industrial design
firm, the interactive portfolio allowed it to inexpensively develop and duplicate
an animated, futuristic
"database" of projects.
Design, 3-D and programming, David Karam; animator, Gigi Biederman;
sound, Tom Bland,
Gravitech Music.

These images (and others
throughout the next six
pages) are post tool's story
and identity.

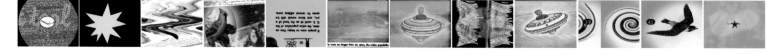

left
David, Gigi and Esme. Photography, Olivier Laude; illustrator, Eugenio de Arnal.

below
Interactive press kit for Warner Bros. Records, Burbank, CA. "Stone Free: A Tribute to Jimi Hendrix," distributed on floppy disk and through America Online, the kit features 13 bands, including the Cure, the Pretenders and Belly covering Hendrix songs, some original Hendrix material, plus a virtual acid trip. Designers, illustrators and programming, post tool; photography, Jim Marshall and Ed Caraeff.

below
Interactive press kit for Lush's album, *Split*; Warner Bros. Records. The kit's information is delivered rather than a set of menus. It contains three songs, liner notes, band photos and interviews promoting the CD, and is distributed by floppy disk and through America Online. Designers, illustrators and programmers, post tool; logotype, V23; photography, Richard Caldicott and Melodie McDaniel.

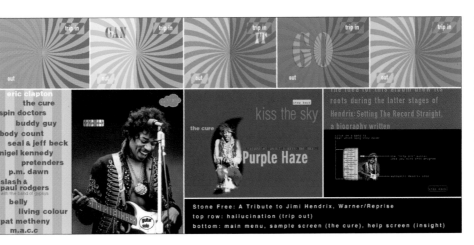

below
Logo and "Virtual Barker" for Electric Carnival, an interactive technology exhibit at Lolapallooza, sponsored by Interval Research. The tent of technology allowed concert attendees to make digital art or just look at displays of new media. Logo, illustrator and animator, Gigi Biederman; video montage, post tool.

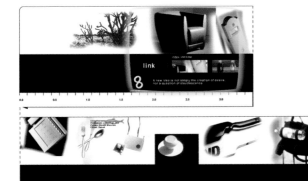

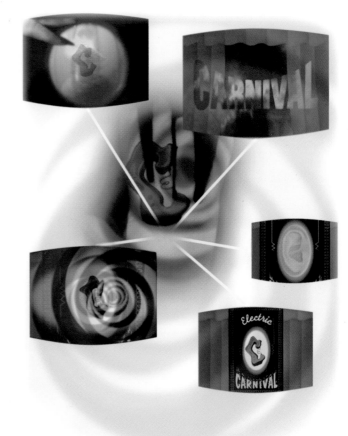

Prototype for an interactive television station, "Tele TV," for the video production company, 2-Headed Monster, Hollywood, CA. The environment houses television, interactive advertisement, video-on-demand, educational programming, surf channel, info-tainment (paid advertisement disguised as programming), web access and teleconferencing. The pro-totype was used as a demonstration about future medium for a lecture at the AIGA conference in Seattle. Design, 3-D and programming, David Karam; type, Gigi Biederman; sound, Tom Bland, Gravitech Music.

below
Prototype for a children's interactive "natural wonders" kiosk at the Denver Zoo, CO. The focus was to teach that there is an association between scientific and poetic information, and that animals communicate. Animation and design, Gigi Biederman; design and programming, David Karam; sound, Tom Bland, Gravitech Music.

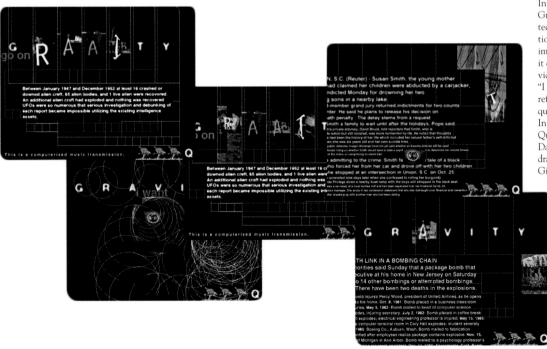

left
Interactive press kit for Gravity, a San Francisco technopop band. A collection of "news of the week" images from the Internet, it displays both sound and video for the band's single, "I Wonder Why," and reflects the docu-drama qualities of the song. Interface designer and Quicktime animator, David Karam; circle drawing screen designer, Gigi Biederman.

below
Watches for Swatch, Milan, Italy. One is part of a series on color blindness. The other is on a transparent band with silk-screened veins. Five of the seven watches prototyped were selected.
Designers/Illustrators, post tool.

bottom left
Christmas mailer for Organic Online, a web-site developer in San Francisco, CA.
Designer/Illustrator, Gigi Biederman.

bottom right
Package design for Electric Hollywood, Hollywood, CA. "Ambulance, an Electronic Novel" is a horror story. A serial killer masquerading as an ambulance driver picks up unsuspecting "twenty-somethings." The novel is usually sold at book stores by the register.
Collage and design, post tool.

left
Identity for Gravitech Music, San Francisco, CA. As a company that composes and does sound design, the illustration shows a press sheet that contains 10 separate elements for its identity, including cards, mailing labels, disk labels, a bumper sticker and a video label.
Designer/Illustrator, David Karam.

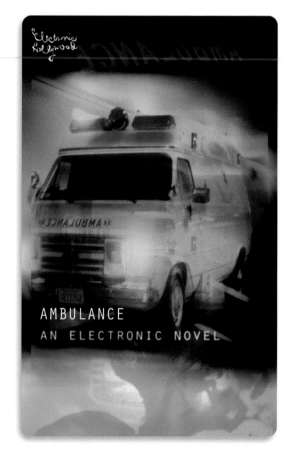

right
Logo for Daypunch, San Francisco, CA. One component of an identity system for a company that creates and markets a calendar based on old-fashion punch boards. The logo's rooster was found on an old fruit crate and was re-shaped and colored. Other identity materials include brochures, product graphics, and a website.
Designers, post tool.

above
Self-promotional playing card to include with correspondence.

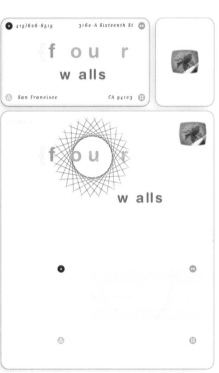

left
Packaging and identity for A.R.M. Around Moscow, a documentary film about the American-Russian Matchmaking service. Four times a year, Ron Rollband brings 15 American men to Moscow to meet over 500 potential Russian brides. The design was used as the video cassette cover and for the 1994 Whitney Biennial Catalog.
Design and type, post tool; directors and editors, Jeanne Finley and Gretchen Stoeltje.

above
Identity for Four Walls, San Francisco, CA, an art gallery that focuses on local artists. Materials include a business card, a promotional postcard, and a card used in the stationery system. Not shown are stationery, envelopes, show catalogs, matchbook catalogs and show invitations.
Collage and design, David Karam; photography and illustrations, various.

Rebeca Méndez

Principal: Rebeca Méndez
Year Founded: 1989
Size of Firm: 1 +
Key Clients: Art Center
College of Design
Graduate and Academic
Publications, The Getty
Center for The History of
Art and Humanity, go2net,
Monacelli Press, Rice
University Architecture
Department, Swatch.

1023 Garfield Ave.
South Pasadena, CA 91030
818˙403 2122

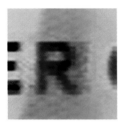

ebeca Méndez handed her pupils on the last day of the term before summer break a score keeping form for a rifle range. In the middle of the bull's-eye she vertically printed the following quotations: "Remember: [...] the graphic designer is a participant in the delivery of the message, not just a translator [...] Objective communication is enhanced by deferred meanings, hidden stories and alternative interpretations. Meanings are as important as materials." Méndez, born and raised in Mexico City, is an honors graduate of Art Center College of Design in Pasadena, and became its design director in 1991. As a designer for an educational institution, Méndez has been acutely concerned with issues of identity. She developed a graphic identity for the college that is recognizable but not fixed: "The identity of an institution is no different from that of a person. Some components remain static, like a backbone, but identity should be dynamic, continually evolving. Cultural institutions in particular need to allow for that." Méndez left the Art Center's Design Office earlier this year to devote more time to teaching, fine art and started her own design studio in a partnership with Bryan Rackleff.

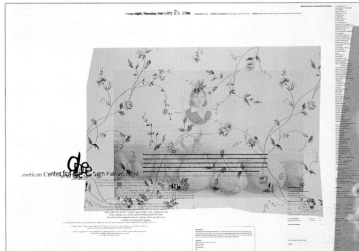

top and right
Poster to promote a presentation by Méndez for the American Center for Design's "Patrons Night," Chicago, IL. The poster includes imagery from her fine art videos, installations and letterpress work. Her lecture focused on the construction and de-construction of identity through boundaries, both at an individual and and institutional level. "These boundaries by which we understand our place within society are largely delineated by the pathways of rational and promiscuous systems of power and socialization. What is most important in this is that these systems of power and ordering are so ingrained so as to appear unquestionable. They, to a large extent, form the lens by which the world is made visible to us."
Designer/video image/ letterpress print/typography/ photography,
Rebeca Méndez.

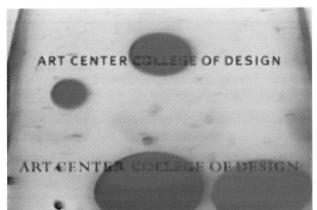

left
Multimedia installation including interactive work by students attending Art Center College of Design. This installation was conceived to expand the presence of Art Center into the East Coast. Two 12-by-16 foot video projections were looped to play day and night; one projected onto the front window of the art gallery, interactive art, video art and several three-dimensional student pieces.

Curator/Director/Producer/ Editor, Rebeca Méndez and Jessica Bronson; director of photography, Celine Fitzpatrick; title design, Méndez; assistant title designer, Thomas Müller.

right
Poster for The Getty Center for the History of Art and the Humanities, Santa Monica, CA. The center is dedicated to advanced research in the history of art—reexamining art and artifacts in order to "reassess" its importance to the social sciences and humanities. To represent the idea of "reassessment," Méndez chose a piece from the Getty's collection by Fluxus artist George Brecht. The piece states, "This sentence is weightless" in negative letterforms cut from aluminum sheets.

"Language has no physical weight, yet the meaning of words can, of course, have profound weight. The photo of the man facing the horizon, (Western Avenue and Pico Boulevard, 1903) struck me as a historical moment full of hope seeming to anticipate the future. The overall design emphasizes openness, which I believe to be an essential requisite for scholarly inquiry." Designer, Rebeca Méndez; photography, John Kiffe and Jobe Benjamin.

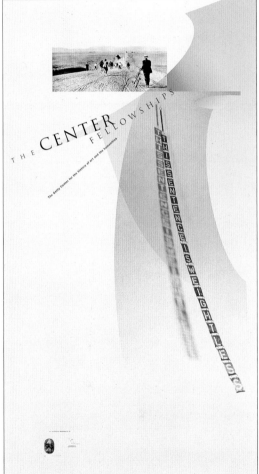

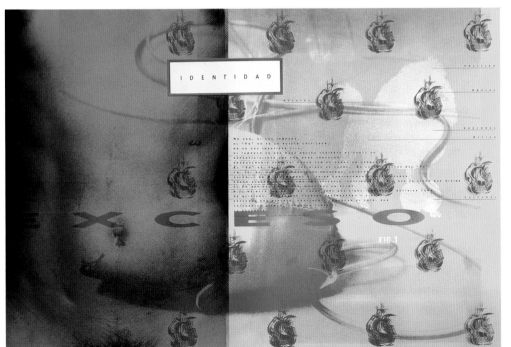

left
Poster for the Second International Biennial of the Poster, Mexico City. The poster was one of 40 at the international invitational collection with the theme, "America Now, 500 Years Later." Méndez said she explored issues of identity for the poster.
"The development of an identity is a complex process, and any identity, whether it is cultural, personal, national, racial, political, or all of them together, is in constant state of change and mutation. The torso represents the individual in both its strength and vulnerability. By reducing Columbus' ship to a decorative wallpaper element, I question and dilute the celebration of the so-called 'conquest.' The faint silhouette of the Poodle serves as example of how species ownership limits, traps and distorts identity. What I see and feel around me is an excess of categorization. But in Trinh T. Minh-ha's words, 'Despite out desperate, eternal attempt to separate, contain, and mend, categories always leak.'"
Designer, Rebeca Méndez.

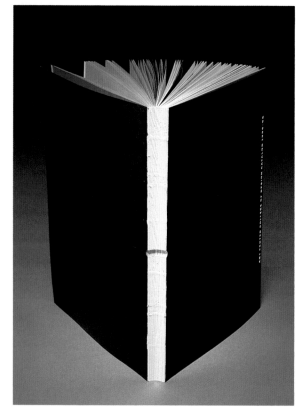

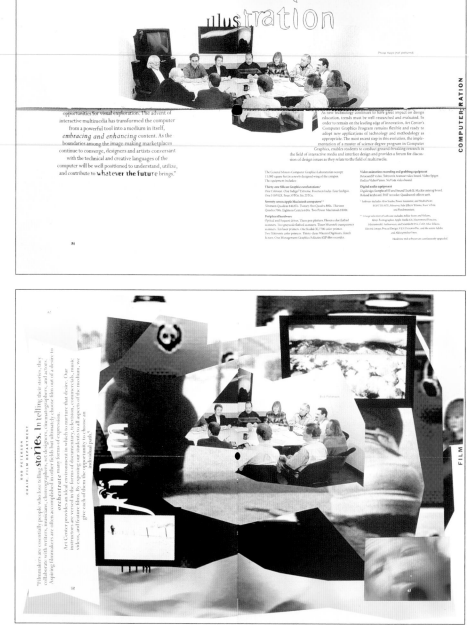

Catalog for the Art Center College of Design, Pasadena, CA. Because the design practice and culture were in a transition at the school, the sense of ambivalence—of being at the threshold—became the vision for the catalog. The history, both of Art Center's publications, and graphic design, is re-examined in order to extract its essential concepts. "New media and technology are having dramatic cultural consequences; thus, we had to consider that this might be our last printed catalog. The idea of a reconfigured book, one that could be literally 'broken,' emerged. By perforating the pages horizontally, we suggested the idea of a nonlinear narrative. Formally the book, although classical in its configuration, has an unfinished or half-destroyed appearance, condensing its life cycle. The perforation bisects the headlines to identify specific areas of study, creating hybrid words and opening our minds to the inter-disciplinary and multi-disciplinary environments at the college. The

typography momentarily forgets its classical roots and its autonomy. We randomly "distressed" certain elements of the typography so that its fluidity is revealed as it is affected by surrounding elements. The design reflects a range of expressions, from the sublime to the ridiculous. Our use of images reveals another transition—from the continuous spatial and tonal variations of analog pictures to the discrete elements of digital imagery—addressing the question of what is an 'original' versus and 'exact replica.' In Abbott Miller's words, 'The catalog seems like a culmination of developments in design over the last few years...[It] speaks out loudly as a kind of summation.'"

Creative Director, Stuart Frolick; design director, Rebeca Méndez; designer, Darin Beaman; associate designer, Chris Haaga; photography, Steven A. Heller; art, Art Center students.

above

Titled "The will of the potato," this letterpress print is one of a series of fine art works in which Méndez primarily explores the tensions implicit in social contracts between individuals and institutions, and how these "agreements" form identity. "One issue that permeates this work is the fine line dividing nurture and control," Méndez says. Central in all her fine art works is the potato, a metaphor for the human being. "The potato is the lowest common denominator of vegetables and it holds energy within." The potato in the letterpress print is wrapped in latex, a simulation of skin, and hangs suspended from a thread. "Two things could happen, depending on the 'past' of the potato," she says. "Either it 'dies' and rots inside the pouch, or it grows roots and eventually punctures and breaks free from the latex.

right

Book for the Art Center College of Design, Pasadena, CA. The book offers current and prospective fine art students a range of realistic options and practical advice. "My approach to this design focused in communicating solidarity and trust. The model employed for the aesthetic frame for the book was the visual language of a governmental institution. Size, cover material, and round corners reference the passport. Art information presented throughout this aesthetic reveals at a very subtle level of inherent tensions between an individual and an institution: surrendering/ control; freedom/confinement; flesh/metal; art/work." Designer, Rebeca Méndez; production, Ellie Eisner; photography, various.

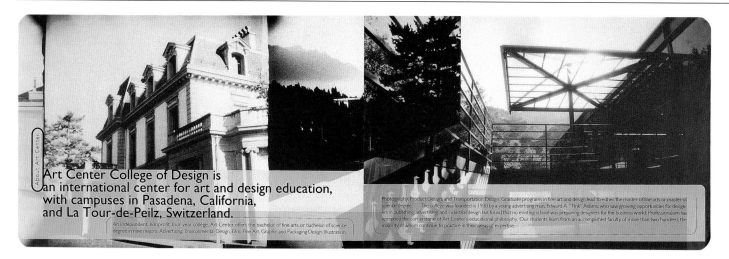

Art Center College of Design is an international center for art and design education, with campuses in Pasadena, California, and La Tour-de-Peilz, Switzerland.

An independent, nonprofit, four-year college, Art Center offers the bachelor of fine arts or bachelor of science degree in nine majors: Advertising, Environmental Design, Film, Fine Art, Graphic and Packaging Design, Illustration,

Photography, Product Design, and Transportation Design. Graduate programs in fine art and design lead to either the master of fine arts or master of science degree.   The college was founded in 1930 by a young advertising man, Edward A. "Tink" Adams, who saw growing opportunities for designers in publishing, advertising, and industrial design but that no existing school was preparing designers for the business world. Professionalism has remained the cornerstone of Art Center's educational philosophy. Our students learn from an accomplished faculty of more than two hundred, the majority of whom continue to practice in their areas of expertise.

Product Design

C. Martin Smith, Chair, Product Design Department

"Product designers today are turning away from the austere modernism of the last few decades and creating products that are more expressive in their visual language. Art Center has played an important role in these developments. Our Product Design majors learn to address current industry and consumer needs through the development of strong conceptual abilities, perseverance in problem solving, and high standards of craftsmanship. With these qualities, our graduates are ready to contribute to a complex, constantly changing world by designing products that embody the promise of the future."

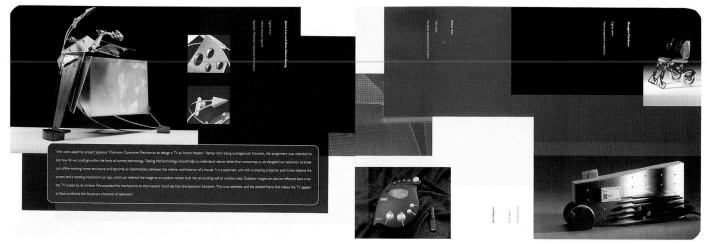

"We were asked by project sponsor Thomson Consumer Electronics to design a TV as 'home theater.' Rather than being outrageously futuristic, the assignment was intended to see how far we could go within the limits of current technology. Feeling that technology should help us understand nature rather than cocooning us, we designed our television to break out of the existing home enclosure and become an intermediary between the interior and exterior of a house. It is a stationary unit with a rotating projector and mirror behind the screen and a rotating mechanism on top, which can redirect the image to an outdoor screen built into an existing wall or window area. Outdoor images can also be reflected back onto the TV screen by its mirrors. We exposed the mechanisms so that viewers could see how the television functions. The lunar aesthetic and the slanted frame that makes the TV appear to float symbolize the illusionary character of television."

above
Catalog for the Art Center College of Design, Pasadena, CA. "The catalog is the single most important recruitment and marketing piece that Art Center produces (biannually)," Méndez says. "The reader's sensory experience is heightened through the book's elasticity; it yields and bends to the touch. The layering of images on the cover and throughout adds spatial depth and allows several points of view to exist simultaneously. "
Designer, Rebeca Méndez; associate designer, Darren Namaye and Darin Beaman; production, Ellie Eisner; photography, Steven A. Heller.

right
Poster for an international design conference in Kyoto, Japan, Art Center College of Design. "The oval form refers to the resonance of a small stone after it has just been dropped in calm waters," says Méndez. "The stone is a metaphor for the the idea to instigate a third Art Center College of Design after the European and Pasadena campus. The resonance represents the trajectory of an idea. The calligraphy reads Ichigo Ichie: 'One lifetime, one meeting.'"
Creative Director, Rebeca Méndez and Stuart Frolick; designer/art director, Méndez; Zen calligraphy, Nakagima Kosho; photography, Steven A. Heller.

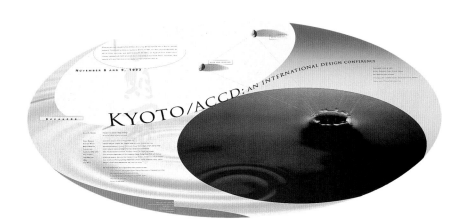

right

A series of art installations, video pieces and digital animation experiments to help Méndez explore thinking in terms of time rather than space. "For a short film conceived as a meditation on control and surrendering, for example, I capture the slow interaction of two colored substances, bright orange potassium permanganate and yellow lemon sherbet, as they slowly melt in water," Méndez says. "A soundtrack of whispers keeps interrupting the scrolling text. *The Malady of Death* by Marguerite Duras. Wrenching in its simplicity—no more complex than a screen saver—the short film demonstrates one instance of frustration of the will of the mind unable to control its own body or that of 'the lover.'" Director/Producer/Editor/ Photography, Rebeca Méndez; AVID technical assistance, Garth Grinde; text, *The Malady of Death*, by Marguerite Duras.

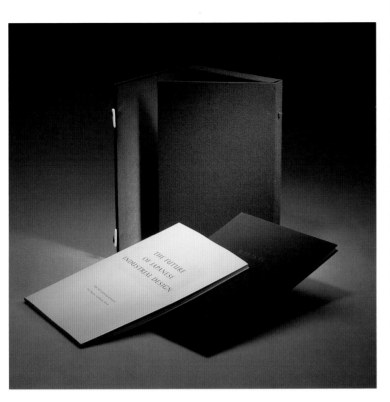

left and above left

Book for the Art Center College of Design. The approach to this design began with an existing book—written and published in 1956 by Art Center's founder, E.A. Adams—and was reproduced without any design alteration. Its companion piece was designed around a set of photographs made during Adams' trip to Japan. The book honors the life recorded in the images' content, as well as the impact of time on the photographs-as objects. "The design suggests the intimate, personal quality of a photo album. It also references the 'archeology' of these particular images, its discoloration with age, its markings—both intentional (handwritten notes, rubber stamps and reproduction codes)—and unintentional, (tears, remnants of taped captions and stains)." Creative Director, Rebeca Méndez and Stuart Frolick; designer, Méndez; producer, Ellie Eisner; photography, various.

Salsgiver Coveney Associates

Principal: Karen Salsgiver
Year Founded: 1983
Size of Firm: 2
Key Clients: The Carnegie
Museum of Art, Champion
International Corporation,
Condé Nast Books,
Ethan Allen, Inc.;
The Juilliard School,
Hampshire Group, Limited;
Harvard Business School
Press, Lincoln Center for
the Performing Arts, Inc.;
MasterCard International,
The New York Public
Library, Random House, Inc.

Four Birch Road
Westport, CT 06880
203 454 1056

Salsgiver Coveney Associates' work is clear, elegant and personal—dense with beauty, meaning and intelligence. For Karen Salsgiver, the creative process evolves out of the distilling of complex material and messages—creating graphically simple work that is functional, but still integrates engaging playfulness and humanity. Since 1983, this way of thinking has earned the firm prestigious awards and a devoted clientele in areas encompassing the arts, publishing, finance, home furnishings, fashion and the paper industry.

left
Envelope papers *Fact Finder* and swatchbooks for Champion International Corporation, Stamford, CT. Envelope paper is more of a commodity than premium paper, and therefore more difficult to differentiate from grade-to-grade and mill-to-mill. To solve this, these swatchbooks create an individual identity for each paper using a die-cut icon on the cover to represent the product's main strengths.
Designers, Karen Salsgiver and Laura Howell.

above and opposite page
Annual report for The Juilliard School, New York, NY. This is the third in a series of four reports that use progressively changing formats, to represent the growth and evolution of education at the school. Designers, Karen Salsgiver and Cathleen Mitchell; writers, Lynne Rutkin, Karen Raven and Jon Goldman.

left
Karen Salsgiver.
Photography,
Don Hamerman.

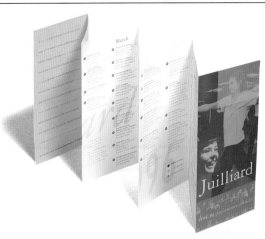

above
Calendar for The Juilliard
School, New York, NY.
The design ties in with the
annual report (left), and
the information is sorted
by many categories in a
simple way. The calendar
informs faculty, board
members, donors, members
of the community and
prospective students about
workshops/performances.
Designers, Karen Salsgiver
and Laura Howell.

below left
Exhibition catalog for the
New York Public Library,
New York, NY. The book
documents the show's
objects and manuscripts in
a way that is sympathetic
with the character of
Cummings' life and writing.
Designers, Karen Salsgiver,
Laura Howell and
Angela Voulangas.

bottom right
Annual report papers
promotion for Champion
International Corporation,
Stamford, CT. The portfolio
contains dummies of beau-
tiful paper combinations.
Designer, Karen Salsgiver.

below
Paper promotion for
Champion International
Corporation, Stamford, CT.
Research into the fabric
hopsack, which inspired the
texture of the paper, lead to
a rich history of hops and
brewing going as far back as
the Egyptians. The solution
packages an abridged history
in a "hops sack."
Designer, Karen Salsgiver;
writers/researchers,
Salsgiver and Robin Sanders.

right
Annual report for the
Lincoln Center Consolidated
Corporate Fund, New York,
NY. By surrounding Lincoln
Center's central plaza fountain with icons representing
each constituent, this cover
unifies the ten performing
arts organizations which
benefit from gifts to the Fund.
The fountain is then used
as an icon to represent the
Fund throughout a compre-
hensive identity program.
Designers, Karen Salsgiver
and Laura Howell;
illustrator, Anthony Russo.

below
Interactive CD-ROM
catalog for Ethan Allen,
Inc., Danbury, CT. The
screens show the breadth
and depth of the product
line in stores where displays
are limited.
Designers, Karen Salsgiver
and Laura Howell.

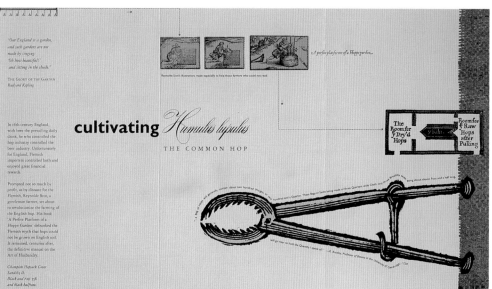

below
Comprehensive program of wall panels, brochures, certificates and signage for Ethan Allen Sleep Shop, Danbury, CT. The designs create a soft, restful environment for testing and purchasing bedding. Designer, Karen Salsgiver; photography, Gentl & Hyers.

right
Book design for Houghton Mifflin Company, Boston, MA. The book weaves together the impressions of two friends who visited three Italian islands—one who rendered hers in words, the other who rendered hers in photographs. Designer, Karen Salsgiver; writer, Barbara Grizzuti Harrison; photography, Sheila Nardulli.

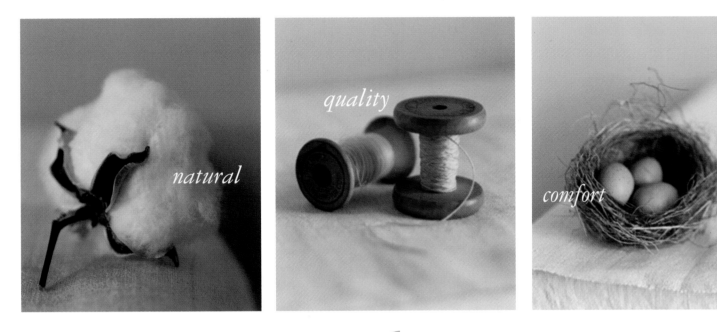

natural

quality

comfort

tables & chairs

left
Brochures for Ethan Allen. Two covers from a series designed to work as a system of small posters in lucite holders throughout the store. Each brochure serves a product line, and includes a logo which carries through to a system of in-store banners, advertising and hang tags. Designer, Karen Salsgiver; photography, Ethan Allen Photo Studio.

above
Store directory for Ethan Allen. The hand-held guide helps to simplify shopping. It combines a store map, shopping/services guide and order card. Designer, Karen Salsgiver.

right
Logos and wordmarks for Ethan Allen. Designer, Karen Salsgiver.

CLOCKWORKS™

the *contour* line

right
Self-promotional notecard.
Designers, Karen Salsgiver
and Laura Howell.

far right
Annual report for The
Hampshire Group, New
York, NY. The design is
executed in one color
throughout, with elegant
use of tints and typography.
Designers, Karen Salsgiver
and Laura Howell.

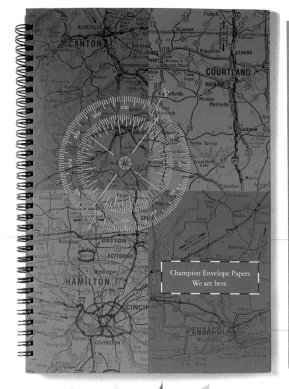

above
Capability piece for
Champion International
Corporation, Stamford, CT.
This book, which covers
the company's large line of
envelope papers and its work
in setting environmental
standards, uses locations
where envelopes might
travel to highlight and
differentiate the strengths
of each grade.

Designers, Karen Salsgiver
and Cathleen Mitchell;
writers/researchers,
Salsgiver, Robin Sanders
and Jon Goldman.

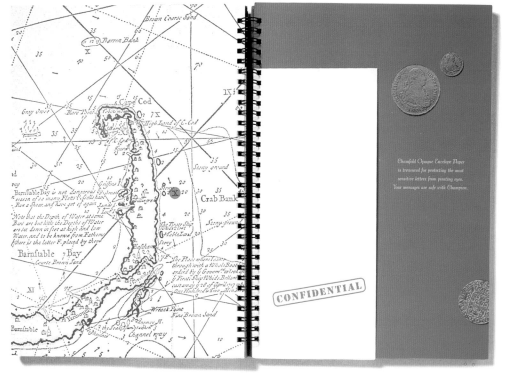

right and below right
Catalog and invitation for an exhibition of an alphabet designed by 12 graphic designers for Champion International Corporation, Stamford, CT. The deck of alphabet cards was designed as a memento for the Aspen Design Conference's opening exhibit. Designers, Karen Salsgiver and Laura Howell; "Y" card shown, designed by Woody Pirtle; writer/researcher, Karen Salsgiver.

above
Sales contest announcement and premiums for Champion International Corporation. Designers, Karen Salsgiver and Laura Howell; writer/researcher, Karen Salsgiver.

left
Cookbook design for Random House, Inc., New York, NY. Although conceived as a book for *Gourmet* readers, the design was a rather radical departure from the magazine, and was used to reach out to a broader audience. Designers, Karen Salsgiver and Laura Howell.

Segura Inc.

Principal: Carlos Segura
Year Founded: 1991
Size of Firm: 6

1110 North Milwaukee Avenue
Chicago, IL 60622-4017
773 862 5667
www.SEGURA-INC.com
www.T26FONT.com

egura Incorporated was born from the frustrations of Carlos Segura's 13-year career in advertising—opening its doors in January 1991 to pursue design and its tangible and personal possibilities. Drawn to the print medium, all forms of materials were based on three basics: typography, papers and fine art. Fueled by curiosity, experimentation was a primary direction in all efforts leading to the development and creation of [T-26], a new digital type foundry, making its debut in the fall of 1994. Another form of expansion has been multimedia, web site and interactive presentations—all with the philosophy that, "communication that doesn't take a chance, doesn't stand a chance."

above
Header card and WaxTin labels for the wireframe XXX Snowboards wax display, (Lake Bluff, IL).

above right
Imagery, stationery and identity explorations for MTV Networks, NY, NY.

right
Sticker for Q101 Radio, Chicago, IL. Part of a campaign of assorted images used in all stationery, collateral, postcards, promotional items, give-aways and advertising.

below
Lid designs for the 1997
Apple Powerbook's new
removable clear panel,
Cupertino, CA.

bottom
Part of a series of stickers
and CD for [T-26].
Compact Discs for Tooth
& Nail Records' Klank
release, Seattle, WA.

right/from top to bottom
Cover for the 1996 LowRes
Digital Film Festival; Klank
CD; cover of the 1995
product catalog for TVT
Records; Nanotek Warrior

Interactive CD-ROM for
Virgin Interactive. Card
announcing the distribution
of [T-26] fonts in South Africa
through CyberGraphics.

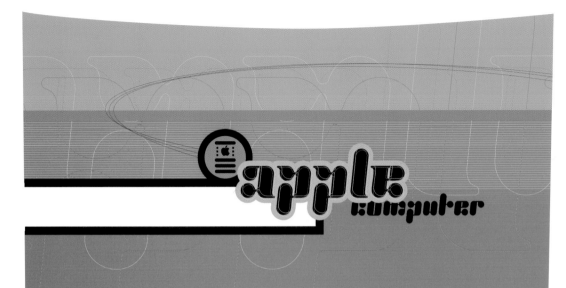

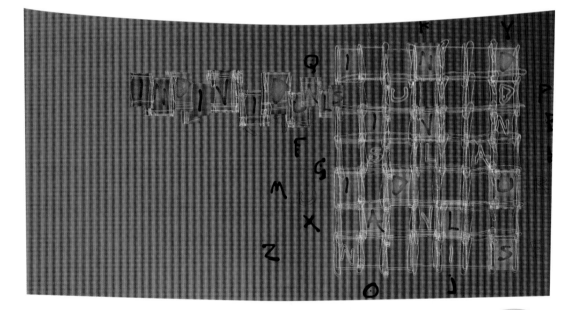

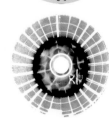

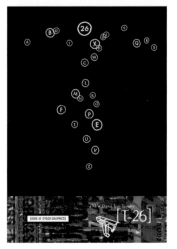

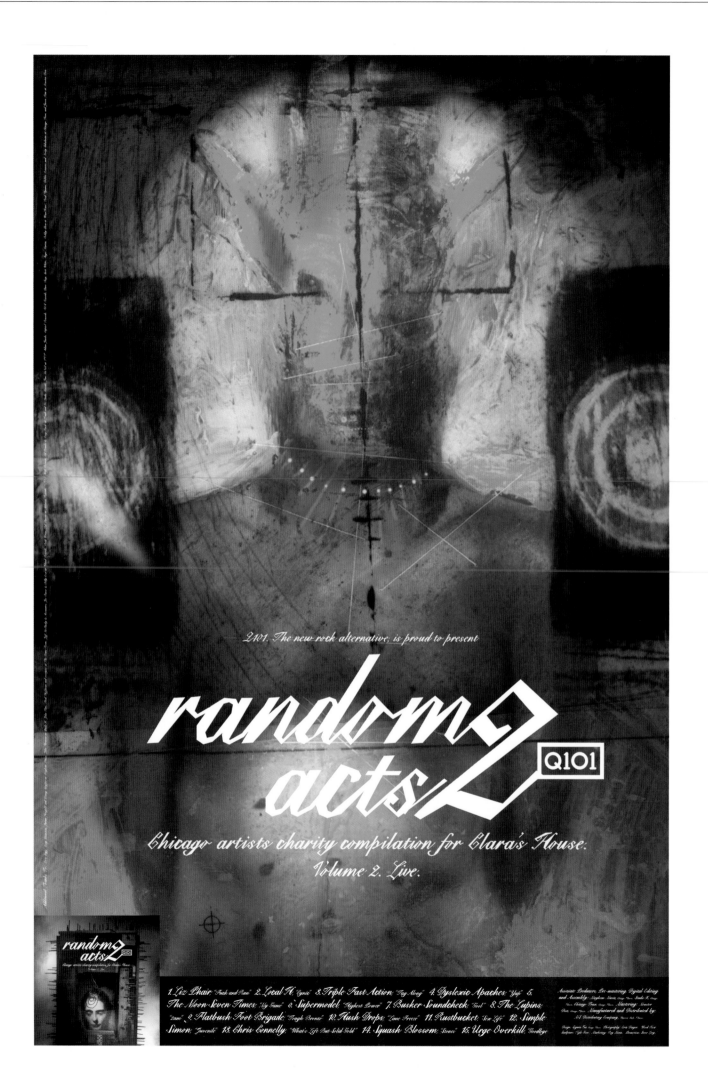

top row

left: Invitation and CD for
Q101 Radio, Chicago, IL.
"Alternative" is a promotion
for a free trip to Italy to see
the Red Hot Chili Peppers.
right: CD promotion for
Q101 Radio, (poster on
opposite page).

"Random Acts 2," featuring
Chicago bands, is a benefit
for Clara's House, a battered
woman's shelter.

middle row

left: "Thickface," a
CD-ROM of background
images sold through
[T-26] Type Foundry.
right: Generic CD cover
used for promotional
releases by A&M Records,
(Hollywood, CA).

bottom row

left: Box set for WaxTrax!
& TVT Records, (NY).
"Blackbox" is one of three
limited-edition compilations
to celebrate the label's
13-year history.
right: CD cover and design
for Psykosonic,
TVT/WaxTrax! Records.
"Unlearn" is the first single
from the band's second LP.

A series of stickers for *The Alternative Pick*, NY, NY. Part of the 1996 campaign developed for the national creative sourcebook, the campaign consists of the book, a limited edition box set, a calendar, four posters, bookmarks, pencils, assorted cards, a t-shirt and shipping carton.

Siebert Design Associates

Principal: Lori Siebert,
Steve Siebert
Year Founded: 1987
Size of Firm: 10
Key Clients: Bath & Body
Works, Cincinnati,
Comtemporary Arts
Center, Empire Berol,
Ensemble Theatre of
Cincinnati, Formica
Corporation, Hewlett
Packard, How Magazine,
LensCrafters, Limited Too,
Marketing to Kids Report.

1600 Sycamore Street
Cincinnati, OH 45210
513 241 4550

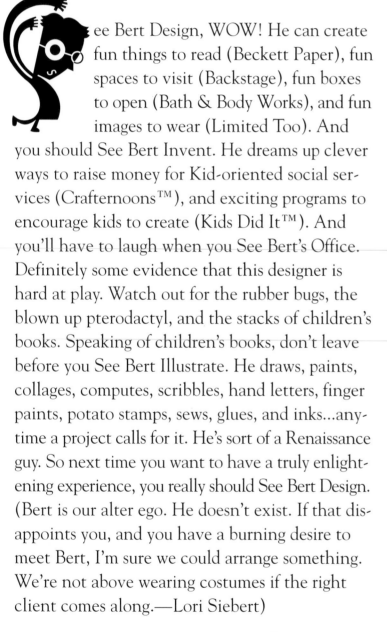

ee Bert Design, WOW! He can create fun things to read (Beckett Paper), fun spaces to visit (Backstage), fun boxes to open (Bath & Body Works), and fun images to wear (Limited Too). And you should See Bert Invent. He dreams up clever ways to raise money for Kid-oriented social services (Crafternoons™), and exciting programs to encourage kids to create (Kids Did It™). And you'll have to laugh when you See Bert's Office. Definitely some evidence that this designer is hard at play. Watch out for the rubber bugs, the blown up pterodactyl, and the stacks of children's books. Speaking of children's books, don't leave before you See Bert Illustrate. He draws, paints, collages, computes, scribbles, hand letters, finger paints, potato stamps, sews, glues, and inks...anytime a project calls for it. He's sort of a Renaissance guy. So next time you want to have a truly enlightening experience, you really should See Bert Design. (Bert is our alter ego. He doesn't exist. If that disappoints you, and you have a burning desire to meet Bert, I'm sure we could arrange something. We're not above wearing costumes if the right client comes along.—Lori Siebert)

right
T-shirt graphic to use on baby merchandise for Limited Too, Columbus, OH. The illustrative style is fun, whimsical and colorful, as well as educational. Designers, Lori Siebert and Lisa Ballard.

top
Promotional materials for Howard Paper, Dayton, OH. To elevate the perception of a "workhorse" sheet, the piece was designed with rich illustration and photography. The theme tied in directly to the objective, including extraordinary stories of how everyday things, like velcro, buttons, etc, came to be. Designers, Lori Siebert and Lisa Ballard.

above
Promotional materials for Beckett paper, Hamilton, OH. A tabloid-sized book was created to launch a new grade of paper that featured a mix of strong illustration and photography. Each spread represented a different emotion. The die cut "X" for "Expression" is through the center of the book. Shown are Pol Turgeon, Doug Fraser and Paul Elledge.

Designers, Lori Siebert, Diane Gliebe, Lisa Ballard and Joe Stryker; writer, Bob Guard; illustrator/photography, various.

left
Left to right: (back row) Lisa Ballard, Ben Meyers, Barb Matulionis, Michelle Daniel, Amy Ollberding and Diane Gliebe; (front row) Steve Siebert, Lori Siebert, Kevin Armstrong and Nick Gliebe; (not pictured) Lori Maechling. Photography, Dane Heithaus of Kauck Productions.

below
Series of "Kenzie Dolls" created to auction at Crafternoons, a fundraiser for three children's charities. Twenty-two dolls, originally drawn by 6-year-old McKenzie Siebert, were made with vintage fabrics and accessory pieces, and brought in a $1700 profit to donate. Because of its success, more dolls were made called "Odd Ball Dolls." Designers, Lori and McKenzie Siebert; sewing assistants, Michelle Daniel, Marcia Short and Sandy Weinstein.

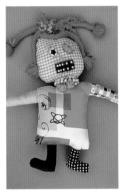

far left and left
Redesign of *HOW Magazine*, F&W Publications, Cincinnati, OH. The magazine wanted a distinct look without losing freshness with each issue. A cleaner look was made based on the exploration of grids. Although many elements are unchanging from issue to issue, it has greater allowance to express the "*How*" language. Designers, Lori Siebert, Lisa Ballard and Nick Gliebe; photography, Guildhaus Photography.

left,
Brochures and collateral for Hewlett Packard, San Diego, CA. Using a "partnering" theme, all applications—from presentation slides and logo development to signage and mailers—were created for the company's Developer's Conference. Designers, Lori Siebert, Lisa Ballard, Barb Matulionis and David Carroll; illustrator, Ballard.

far left,
Using the partnering theme again, this logo was developed for the Hewlett Packard Developer's Conference in San Antonio, TX. Designer/illustrator, Lisa Ballard.

right
Identity and core signage pieces for a city block directly across from Cincinnati's new Aronoff Center for the Performing Arts. The client was Michael Schuster Associates, Cincinnati, OH. Each totem along the street includes a humorous or interesting anecdote from Cincinnati's performing arts history. Figures that top the poles alternate between dancers, actors and musicians. Designers, Lori Siebert, Lisa Ballard, Nick Gliebe and Ben Meyers; illustrators, Ballard and Hank Osuna.

top left and top right
Keepsake pieces for the Contemporary Arts Center, Cincinnati, OH. The student "diaries" were made for participants of Vital Vision, an educational outreach program where visiting artists work with kids in several inner-city schools. Created as an interactive piece, questions are asked that relate to the artist's work while leaving space for the kids to write and draw. The Joyce Scott piece even has a weaving loom. Designers, Lori Siebert and Michelle Daniel; illustrators, Joyce Scott and Carrie Mai Weems.

above
Poster to advertise the Over-the-Rhine Heritage Festival for the Chamber of Commerce, Cincinnati, OH. The festival, referencing the turn of the century, rededicated a gazebo within the park and celebrated with antique cars, sousa bands and period costumes. The poster's layout is reminiscent of announcements and ads from the time. Designer/illustrator, Lori Siebert.

right
Poster for a fundraising lecture about angels given by a noted author, St. Catherine Church, Ft. Thomas, KY. The fundraiser needed to raise $7000 for a new church roof. The folk-art approach to the subject was atypical of Renaissance-like cherubs, making it stand out; and the fundraiser raised $12,000. Designer/calligrapher, Lori Siebert; illustrator, Amy Butler.

right and left
Stationary and identity for a contemporary film company, Mondo Syndicato, Cincinnati, OH. To create an identity as unique and memorable as the name itself, the constructivism-style logo and the image of the mafia-like central character reflects the attitude of the company's name. Designer/Illustrator, Lisa Ballard.

left
Holiday room sprays for Bath & Body Works, Columbus, OH. The design coordinated the look of other holiday packages developed by the client, while giving this project its own distinctive design. Designers, Lori Siebert and Lisa Ballard; illustrator, Ballard.

above
Subscription renewal brochure for the Ensemble Theatre of Cincinnati, OH. Created as a direct mail piece, the design looks spontaneous like a scrapbook, with torn ticket stubs and taped photos. Key emotional words within play descriptions are highlighted through size to give the reader an "at a glance" summary. Designer, Lori Siebert and Lisa Ballard; illustrator, David Sheldon.

right
Bath & Body Works Home Store pet products packaging. Printed on recycled paper, the design direction had to mesh with the simplicity of the other packaging within the store and expand on existing illustrations. Designer, Lisa Ballard; illustrators, Ballard and Michael Mabry.

Strokes pens packaging
and display for Northlich
Stolley, LaWarre, agency for
Empire Berol, Brentwood,
TN. The fashion pen
design—targeted at young
girls age 13-19—reflects
handwriting and the variety
of patterns related to the
idea of self expression—
choose a pen according
to your mood.
Designers, Lori Siebert,
Diane Gliebe and Lisa
Ballard; illustrators, Amy
Butler, Janey Wooly,
Siebert, Ballard and Gliebe.

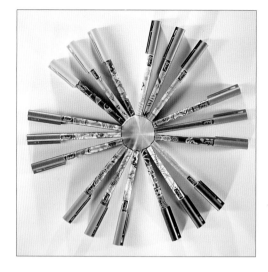

top row
Three-dimensional exhibit totems for Cincinnati Park Board, OH. The icons are like large interlocking puzzles made of foam core, easy to assemble and disassemble. The icons became so popular that Siebert Design is in the process of exploring a product idea based on the design. Designers, Lori Siebert and Lisa Ballard; illustrator, Ballard.

above
Design for an expanded sunglass department for LensCrafters, Cincinnati, OH. Tested in select markets, the expanded environment evokes an attitude of the brands featured in the department. Using a pointillist style, reminiscent of Seurat paintings, a large, panoramic, illustrated mural spans the department, depicting people in a vacation-like setting. Designers, Lori Siebert, Lisa Ballard and Diane Gliebe; architects, Michael Schuster Associates; design directors, Renee Ritter and Lou Beckmeyer; mural illustrator, Robert Felker.

above right
Invitation to a series of fundraisers for kids at risk, organized by Siebert Design. The invitation was designed to look hand done, with a series of individual, colorful pages cut with pinking shears and held together with a tiny clothespin. Auctioned at the event were handmade items made by several "creatives" in the field that visited Siebert Design offices throughout the year, or supporters who sent in pieces. Designer/Illustrator/Calligrapher, Lori Siebert; designer Michelle Daniel.

left
Exhibition catalog for the Contemporary Arts Center, Cincinnati, OH. The 50-page catalog shows several metalworkers. Each image and its type description are placed within "sculptural" shapes. Designers, Lori Siebert, Michelle Daniel and Jeff Fassnacht.

Silvio Design

Principal: Sam Silvio
Year Founded: 1978
Size of Firm: 1
Key Clients: American
Library Association, The
Art Institute of Chicago,
Charles R. Feldstein and
Company, Inc., Houk
Friedman Gallery (New
York), Illinois Facilities
Fund, Lincoln Park Zoo,
Lurie Cancer Center/
Northwestern University,
Ravinia Festival Association.

633 South Plymouth Ct.
Suite 204
Chicago, IL 60605
312 427 1735

"How do you get to design?
Practice. Practice. Practice. Practice. Practice."

Sam Silvio has been principal and sole
design practitioner of Silvio Design, Inc.,
since 1978. He contends that practicing
alone is simply practical: it's how he
protects the strong individuality and
sharp focus of his work. His list of more than one
hundred clients include corporations, non-profit
organizations and educational institutions. He
has produced corporate identities, the gamut of
fundraising and marketing materials, installations,
museum catalogs, and books for children and
adults. He is a member of the American Institute
of Graphic Arts and the American Center for
Design; in 1990 he was invited to join 27 Chicago
designers. Sam Silvio's designs frequently result in
the exact opposite of what's obvious; they often
let humor in on projects that could easily be papered
over with pretension; they reveal the essence of an
idea; and they suggest that, since perfection is
elusive, each new project is an unique opportunity
to keep on practicing.

"Practice.
Practice traveling
without a map."
right
1991 Chicago guidebook
for the American Institute
of Graphic Arts National
Conference, Chicago, IL.
Photography, Alan Shortall.

"Practice.
Practice experimenting
with identities."
right
Logo designs from left to
right: Cattails Press.

The Newhouse Foundation,
(architectural education).

"Writers Live at the
Library," for the American
Library Association
funding project for writers,
Chicago, IL.

"Practice.
Practice working with
groups."
above left
Symposium brochure for
the Lurie Cancer Center,
Northwestern University, IL.

above right
Fundraising campaign for
the Ravinia Festival,
Highland Park, IL.

left
Promotion for the
American Library
Association, Chicago, IL.

"Practice.
 Practice reframing."
opposite page
Catalog for shows of the
work of Bill Brandt, Andre
Kertész, Arthur Siegel,
Brassai, Dorothea Lange,
and Women Photographers
of the 1920s and 1930s.
Houk Friedman Gallery,
New York, NY.

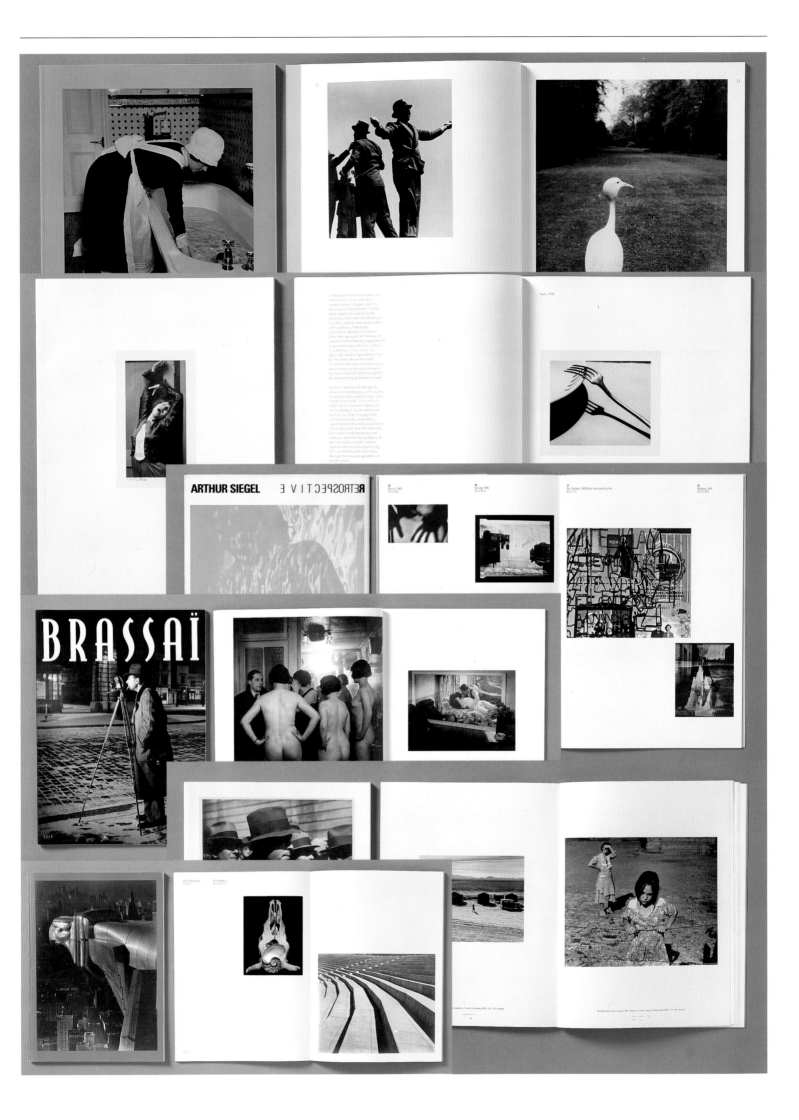

Premier Hospital Alliance.

Opticare eyecare for senior citizens.

Darter Inc., an industrial supply company.

Tyson II, a mall development.

Newman Associates, a film production company.

Roula Associates, an architectural firm.

"Practice.
Practice the unimaginable."
left
Announcement for a book show for the Chicago Chapter of the AIGA Book Show.
Photography, Alan Shortall.

top
Catalog for the Art Institute of Chicago, *Dieter Appelt*.

above
Catalog for the Art Institute of Chicago, *About Place*.

"Practice.
Practice dealing with a range of individuals."
opposite page
Fundraising campaign for the Lincoln Park Zoo, Chicago, IL.

unnatural

freak of
nature

second
nature

Studio Morris

Principals: Jeffrey Morris, Patricia Kovic
Year Founded: 1988
Size of Firm: 12
Key Clients: Reuters, Morgan Stanley, Hot Sox, JMLynne, AIM 21.

55 Vandam Street
Suite 901
New York, NY 10013
212 366 0401

Studio Morris provides the best of both worlds—the personal service and fresh ideas of a small design firm combined with the depth of design and marketing expertise of larger companies. Specializing in integrated communication programs, the firm uses a holistic approach to solve strategic and communication problems. Principals Jeffrey Morris and Patricia Kovic believe these programs are suitable to individual brands and corporations alike. The firm's design philosophy combines Kovic's intuitive working style and Morris' rational approach. Both Morris and Kovic are emphatic in their belief that design is not simply decoration, but a process for solving problems and creating opportunity. This belief accounts for the firm's diversity in clientele—ranging from fashion and contract furnishing to new media and finance. Studio Morris has won numerous design awards, and both principals are visiting professors in the Graduate Design program at Pratt Institute.

above right
Integrated communications program for JMLynne. To re-position the company to compete with other high-end contract wallcovering companies, and to focus on the company's core strengths, the program implemented a tag line, corporate identity, advertising wall covering books and trade show booths. Designers, Jeffrey Morris and Kaoru Sato; photography, Doug Rosa; copywriter, Lisa Friedman.

right
Trademark and wall covering book design for Blumenthal Inc. to increase awareness and improve presentation of the product, the design positioned the company as a leading wall covering supplier. The design of the books' structure also saved the company 40 percent on manufacturing costs. Designer, Jeffrey Morris; marketing consultant, Georgina Walker.

left
Jeffrey Morris.
Photography,
Ray Charles White.

below
Aalto brochure for
International Contract
Furnishings. Created to target consumers rather than
the traditional architect
and designer market, the
existing photography was
combined with hip lifestyle
photography. The rounded
edges of the brochure
reflect the rounded edges of
the furniture.

Designers, Jeffrey Morris
and Patricia Kovic; stock
photography, Photonica;
copywriter, Lisa Friedman.

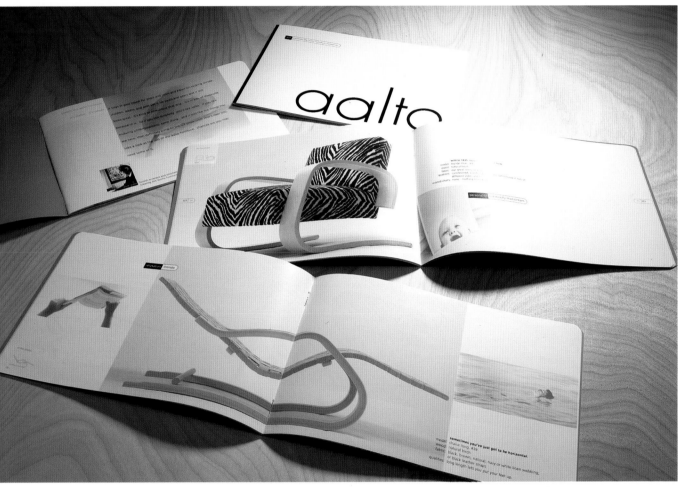

far right
Shopping bags for Unika
Vaev. Printed on translucent,
recyclable plastic, the bag
helped to attract visitors to
the company's showroom
during "Neocon," an indus-
try-wide show in Chicago.
Designers, Jeffrey Morris,
Patricia Kovic and
Kaoru Sato.

right
Catalog sheets for
International Contract
Furnishings. The sheets were
the first implementation of
a marketing communications
system. A totally transparent
design solution allows the
furniture to be the hero. Most
of the furniture is in the
MOMA Design collection.
Designers, Jeffrey Morris,
Patricia Kovic and
Kaoru Sato; photography,
Abby Sadin.

left
Campaign to promote Artwalk for the Coalition for the Homeless, a day where artists in New York open their studios to walking tours. Posters, brochures and advertising explain the tours. A gritty, "from the streets," logo was placed over a diffused rose. The stark contrast between the juxtaposed images communicates its mission.
Designers, Jeffrey Morris and Kaoru Sato.

left
Integrated communications program for Hot Sox Hosiery. This five-year program established a distinctive "voice" and positioning for the company—during which time the company's revenue doubled. The program comprised of a logo, identity system, advertising, packaging, point-of-purchase displays and marketing communications. Designer, Jeffrey Morris; photography, Jaime Phillips.

below
Name development, brand identity and wordmark for Double Take, a franchise of consignment boutiques. The challenge was to take the concept of a second-hand clothing store and make it upscale, fashionable and franchisable. Hang tags were suggested as a way of unifying the merchandise in a store that only carries one of everything.
Designers, Jeffrey Morris and Patricia Kovic.

right
Hosiery package for Ralph Lauren. The project was designed to be sold in a department store environment where it would be competing with other brands, instead of just in the Ralph Lauren stores.
Designer, Jeffrey Morris.

right
Point-of-purchase display for Hot Sox. The display relates to the packaging, as does the advertising and all communication materials. Designer, Jeffrey Morris.

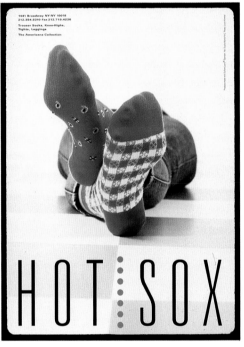

above
"Feet" ad, the first advertisement in the trade campaign showing the new products that the company was designing.
Designer, Jeffrey Morris; photography, Lizzie Himmel.

left
Bus shelter poster for Hot Sox. The image grabs immediate attention as well as advertises that Hot Sox makes animal patterned legwear.
Designer, Jeffrey Morris; photography, Lizzie Himmel.

right
Service mark and brochure for an on-line triage service, Oxford Health Insurance. The objective was to create an identity and communicate to doctors how the program works. The triangle logo design symbolizes the connection between Oxford, doctors and patients. Designers, Jeffrey Morris, Kaoru Sato and Banu Berker; photography, Bard Martin.

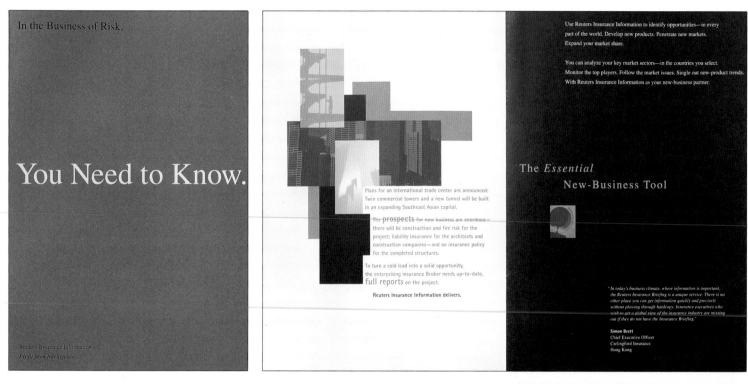

In the Business of Risk.

You Need to Know.

Reuters Insurance Information
Profit from Intelligence.

Use Reuters Insurance Information to identify opportunities—in every part of the world. Develop new products. Penetrate new markets. Expand your market share.

You can analyze your key market sectors—in the countries you select. Monitor the top players. Follow the market issues. Single out new-product trends. With Reuters Insurance Information as your new-business partner.

Plans for an international trade center are announced: Twin commercial towers and a new tunnel will be built in an expanding Southeast Asian capital.

The **prospects** for new business are enormous— there will be construction and fire risk for the project; liability insurance for the architects and construction companies—and an insurance policy for the completed structures.

To turn a cold lead into a solid opportunity, the enterprising insurance Broker needs up-to-date, **full reports** on the project.

Reuters Insurance Information delivers.

The *Essential*
New-Business Tool

"In today's business climate, where information is important, the Reuters Insurance Briefing is a unique service. There is no other place you can get information quickly and precisely without plowing through hardcopy. Insurance executives who wish to get a global view of the insurance industry are missing out if they do not have the Insurance Briefing."

Simon Brett
Chief Executive Officer
Carlingford Insurance
Hong Kong

above
Communications kit for Reuters Insurance Briefing, an on-line business information service for the insurance industry. Specific, real-life examples were used showing the kinds of information available with the services, creating a sense of immediacy and understanding. Designers, Jeffrey Morris and Kaoru Sato; writer, Lisa Friedman.

right
Corporate identity for the Republic New York Corporation, one of the largest financial services corporations in the world. To unify global branding of all subsidiaries and establish a cohesive identity system, the solution could not be flashy. "Understatement" was key to communicating the conservative and stable corporate culture. Designers, Jeffrey Morris, Diane Davidson and Kaoru Sato.

Integrated communications program for Reuters Business Briefing. The on-line service was "branded" and positioned vis-a-vis the competition, which are primarily software companies. The imagery is metaphoric and ethereal, a unique touch for these business-to-business communications.
Designers, Jeffrey Morris, Kaoru Sato and Banu Berker; writer, David Konigsberg.

The product kit consists of various pieces. The image of the hand touching water is for the "Server" version of the product, used to target Managers of Information Services. The back of the pieces used a series of collages, which were also used as an 8-by-10-foot trade show wall.

For more than a century, our primary business has been to gather intelligence from around the world.

Now we deliver it to your desktop.

No matter what your role in business, you need fast, accurate, reliable information. About your industry. About your customers. About your competitors. About the world. Reuters Business Briefing and Reuters Business Alert deliver that intelligence around the clock. For the individual or for the group. On line 24 hours a day.

Call 1.800.383.6335

Reuters, Reuters and the dotted logo are registered trademarks of Reuters Limited in more than 25 countries.

REUTERS
Reuters Business Information
(Intelligence at Your Fingertips)

TeamDesign

Principals: Diann Bissell,
Janet DeDonato and
Bob Grindeland
Year Founded: 1988
Size of Firm: 28
Key Clients: Airborne
Express, Albertson's, AT&T
Wireless, Group Health,
InControl, Kenworth Truck
Company, Microsoft, Plum
Creek Timber Company,
Sierra On-Line, U.S. Bank,
U S WEST.

1809 7th Avenue
Suite 500
Seattle, WA 98101
206 623 1044
www.teamdesign.com

TeamDesign believes that the whole is greater than the sum of its parts—an idea that has allowed it to flourish from a design group of five into a multi-disciplinary firm of 28 in seven years. A leader in Seattle's design community, the firm began with the simple notion that great work comes from a client relationship based on mutual trust and respect. Best known for its work in high-tech industries and annual report design, the firm is adept at making complex information accessible—increasingly through the use of multimedia. By knowing that teamwork draws the best from many individuals into a single vision, TeamDesign has built a national client base and reputation for creative and effective print, electronic and environmental graphic design.

TEAMDESIGN

left
Identity for TeamDesign. The new identity emphasizes collaboration and teamwork while maintaining a witty and whimsical tone. It utilizes six different images, six colors, and each team member has six different business cards. Envelopes, labels and business papers can be interchanged to incorporate use of all six images.
Creative Director, Gary LaComa; designer, Ross Hogin.

top
Promotional materials for Microsoft Corporation, Redmond, WA. The folder, brochure, fact sheets and notebook introduced Microsoft Interactive Television at the National Cable Television Association trade show. A series of photographs were created where its "world" is depicted as a red sphere. "Within Your Grasp" was the theme portrayed by showing the evolution of the technology.
Creative Director, Janet DeDonato; designer, Deborah Brown; photography, Tyler Boley; writer, Bruce Howard.

above
CD-ROM based multimedia presentation for U S WEST Communications, Portland, OR. The presentation served as an introduction to Commercial Video Service, as well as a point of distinction from competing video-transport products. The program works in harmony with supporting printed materials and other training efforts.
Creative Director/ Designer/ Writer, Dale Carlson.

left
From left: Diann Bissell, Bob Grindeland and Janet DeDonato. All portfolio photography taken by David Bell, Studio 3, Inc.

below
Promotional piece for Chateau Ste. Michelle, Woodinville, WA. To introduce the new Canoe Ridge Estate Winery to officers and managers of wine distributors, a poster series was designed around the elements of fine wine—earth, fire, air and water (below right)—which were packaged in a simple, classic portfolio. The posters were so well received that they became available for sale in the winery's gift shop. Creative Director, Janet DeDonato; designer, Renae Bair Dekker; photography, Patience Arakawa and Mel Curtis; illustrators, Dekker and Brett Lloyd.

left
Marketing brochure for Sequent Computer Systems, Inc., Portland, OR. Developed to market it as the single-source solution for advanced telecommunications, the brochure utilizes the photo montage to show its products and services. Creative Director, Gary LaComa; designer, Ross Hogin; photography, William Duke; illustrator, Jeff West.

bottom row
Screen stills from Website and CD-ROM for InfoSource, a database of hardware and software manufacturers worldwide, Microsoft Corporation, Redmond, WA. To present InfoSource as an innovative tool for finding high-performance resources worldwide, graphical interface and multimedia elements were developed through extensive knowledge of human factors, navigational planning and user interface design.

Creative work developed for the interface was shared with the CD-ROM packaging. Creative Director, Dale Carlson; in-house design team, Paula Richards and Rodney Shelden Fehsenfeld; external project team; Tish Hill, Mary Meucci, David Bly, Lewis Chapman, Carl Lipo and Anita Plaschka.

below
Product brochure for Softimage, Microsoft Corporation. To re-introduce a series of high-end software animation products, the design inserted the customers into the images to convey that the products were made from their point of view. A double-gatefold format maximizes the presentation's image, and a custom typeface, created in-house, ties the brochures together.
Creative Director, Gary LaComa; designer, Ross Hogin.

NOMAD
Development Corp

left/opposite page
Identity for Nomad Development, Seattle, WA, a software development corporation for web-based transactions. The design reflects movement, relating to the idea of a nomad. Creative Director, Dale Carlson; designer, Rodney Shelden Fehsenfeld.

right
Logo and campaign materials for the King County Commission for Marketing Recyclable Materials, Seattle, WA. The concept of "Get in the Loop" was developed to refer to the cycle of consumer products and recycling. Campaign materials included posters, brochures, in-store materials, direct mail, signage and newspaper ads. Creative Director, Bob Grindeland; designers, Paula Richards and Karla Chin.

GET IN THE LOOP

BUY RECYCLED ™

below left
Packaging, video labels, invitation and brochure for Multimedia Storytime, an educational tool about multimedia for librarians, Microsoft Corporation, Redmond, WA. The materials were created to look friendly and approachable— not high-tech. Creative Director, Janet DeDonato; designers, Renae Bair Dekker and Brett Lloyd; illustrator, Julie Paschkis.

bottom left
Product brochure for a division of AT&T Wireless Services, Seattle, WA. The cover uses phrases that posed problems about the inability to reach people, while the inside explains the benefits of Cellular Office. A sophisticated look was created to set the product apart from others who try to look more high-tech. Creative Director, Janet DeDonato; designer, Deborah Brown; photography, Darrell Peterson and Warren Mell.

above
Screen stills from a multimedia kiosk to promote Boeing Employees' Credit Union Remote Services products, Tukwila, WA. To show that the service allows employees to spend their time in other ways than banking, animated graphics bounce through key messages and show people involved in leisure-time activities to the tune of Rock Around the Clock. Creative Director, Dale Carlson; designer, Troy Johnson.

MONTAGE

NEW MEDIA TEAMS AND TALENT

above and right
Logo for Montage, a multimedia temporary agency that represents teams and talent for multimedia development, Seattle, WA. The logo is made of letters and pictograms that communicate vision, creative expression, and computer technology. The interchangeable capabilities materials display bright colors and lively images to launch the new company and illustrate its services. Creative Director, Diann Bissell; designer, David Hastings.

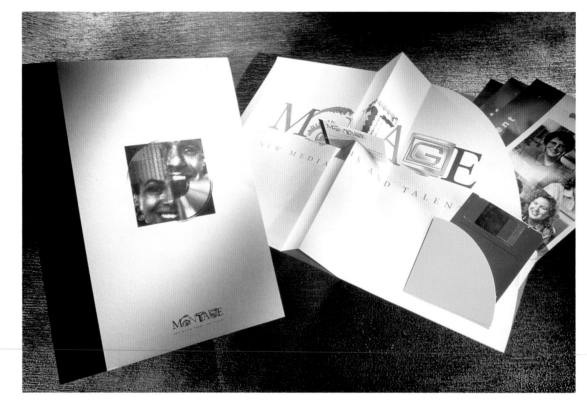

above and right
Corporate identity for Trus Joist MacMillan, Boise, ID. The new identity and graphic standards were created to reflect the benefits of integrated building systems. The logo utilizes a corporate symbol with custom calligraphic type. The mark represents the structural framework of a building combined with a tree to symbolize strength and roots. Creative Director, Diann Bissell; design team, Karla Chin, Renae Bair Dekker, David Hastings, Monica Kaul, Gary Sizemore and Karen Wilson.

NeoRx

left
Identity for NeoRx, Seattle, WA, a bio-pharmaceutical company that specializes in cancer detection and treatment products. The annual report focused on the company's research. A journalistic style of photography was used—minimal lighting and lots of motion while shooting in the lab—to portray the excitement of research. Creative Director, Janet DeDonato; designer, Deborah Brown (annual report), Renae Bair Dekker (identity).

right
Annual report for Immunex Corporation, Seattle, WA. As a leader in oncology, themes for the report focused on research and management. The report makes the link between the business and the science of the company. Through narratives, letters and testimonies, it worked to solidify that the company is a major player in the oncology field. Creative Director, Bob Grindeland; designer, Paula Richards; illustrator, David Hastings.

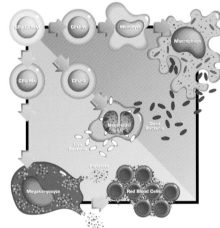

left
Annual report for Plum Creek Timber Company, Seattle, WA. A theme of "Balance" was used to discuss all areas of the company. Split pages support the idea of balance, while each spread has two words representing the two sides that need balance in a particular area, for example, conservation and utilization. Creative Director, Janet DeDonato; designer, Renae Bair Dekker; photography, Walter Hodges and Darrell Peterson.

VSA Partners, Inc.

Principals: Robert Vogele,
Dana Arnett, James Koval,
Curtis Schreiber
Year Founded: 1982
Size of Firm: 25
Key Clients: Ameritech,
Chicago Board of Trade,
The Coca-Cola Company,
Eastman Kodak Company,
Einstein Bros. Bagels,
Harley-Davidson, Inc.,
Northern Telecom,
Playboy Enterprises, Inc.,
Potlatch Corporation,
Time Warner Inc.,
Tyson Foods.

542 South Dearborn
Suite 202
Chicago IL 60605
312 427 6413
www.vsapartners.com

VSA Partners is in the idea business: The firm is founded around the responsibility of expressing ideas in the very best ways possible. Voice is a critical component of any communication design solution. At issue in every assignment is the opportunity to convey a company's position, strategy and purpose with clarity, conviction and power. The firm's heritage and history is design, but the priority is to be communicators who assist business leaders envision change and realize value. Especially skilled in the design and management of annual reports, brand positioning and promotion, and digital communications for corporate clients, VSA Partners is dedicated to one idea: Design, in the right hands, is a very powerful business tool.

CD packaging for Ministry's album, *Filth Pig*, Warner Bros./Sire Records, Los Angeles, CA. To visually create artwork that illustrates the concepts behind the band's songs, it portrays the political climate of America through images that depict the Right-wing movement and its effect on American citizens.

left

Clockwise from top left:
Robert Vogele, James Koval,
Curtis Schreiber and
Dana Arnett
Photography,
François Robert

below

Annual report and catalog
for Harley-Davidson Motor
Company, Milwaukee, WI.
The 1994 annual report
focused on growth and global
expansion of the company.
It sets itself apart by not just
showing bike after bike, but
by selecting and directing
photography that displayed
Harley-Davidson's growth
on a global basis.

The 1995 annual report's
focus was on opportunity.
The report captured and
displayed the many different
lifestyles of the company.
The design, art direction and
production of the 200-page
parts and accessories catalog
was given a theme in keeping
with Harley-Davidson. All
the sections were reorganized
to make it easier to use.

The utilitarian format and
bold, simple photography
made the items in the catalog easier to find, as well as
highlight new products and
collections.

1995 Annual Report.

1996 Genuine Motor
Parts and Genuine Motor
Accessories catalog.

1994 Annual Report.

Website graphics for a local internet provider, XSite, Chicago, IL. The goal was to create top level graphics that load and download fast, are easily understood by the user and each graphic reinforced the XSite name and developed it as a brand.

opposite page
Film and promotional materials for Potlatch Corporation, Cloquet, MN. *Ben Day* is a film featuring the world's greatest designer. It appeals to designers in an unorthodox, but effective way. A print campaign promoted *Ben Day* with pre-event teasers as well as posters and playbills that accompanied the film's showings. The project is considered a "big-thinking" strategy for a paper promotion. Film Writers/Directors, Bob Rice and Dana Arnett.

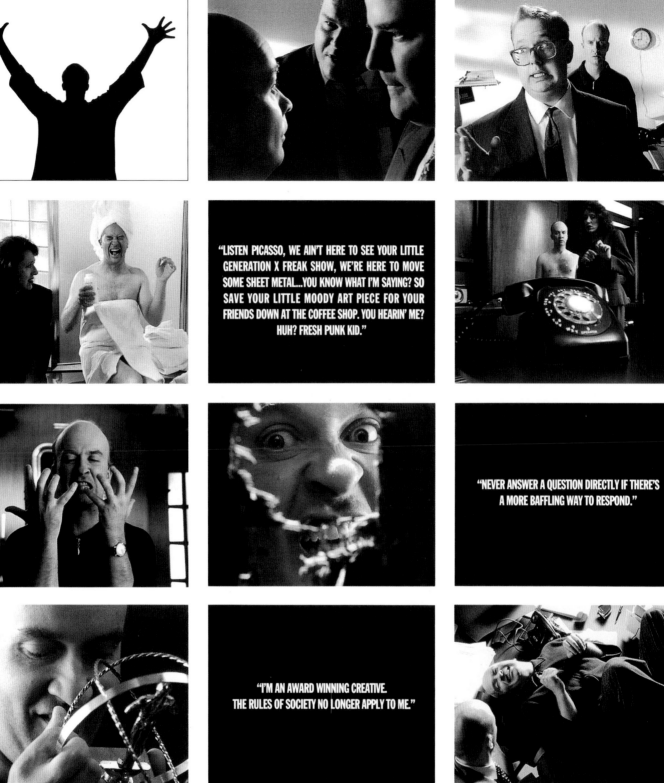

"LISTEN PICASSO, WE AIN'T HERE TO SEE YOUR LITTLE GENERATION X FREAK SHOW, WE'RE HERE TO MOVE SOME SHEET METAL...YOU KNOW WHAT I'M SAYING? SO SAVE YOUR LITTLE MOODY ART PIECE FOR YOUR FRIENDS DOWN AT THE COFFEE SHOP. YOU HEARIN' ME? HUH? FRESH PUNK KID."

"NEVER ANSWER A QUESTION DIRECTLY IF THERE'S A MORE BAFFLING WAY TO RESPOND."

"I'M AN AWARD WINNING CREATIVE. THE RULES OF SOCIETY NO LONGER APPLY TO ME."

"I CAME WITH NOTHING AND THEY BOUGHT IT."

HAVE A BEN DAY

Packaging design for Einstein Bros.. Bagels, Golden, CO. Illustrated by Steven Guarnaccia, the series of 21 cream cheese containers (top and bottom of page) was created as an animated representation of how each flavor tastes. The bagel chips (middle) work both as a unique series and a compliment to the existing, high-energy interior space. Illustrated by Juliette Borda, each flavor is represented as a different character.

opposite page
Annual report for Time Warner Inc., New York, NY. To offer clarity to the company's objectives, it needed a breath of new life and energy into the design of its 1995 annual report. The final design shows the density of Time Warner's assets and properties, but is presented in a colorful, bold and retrievable manner.

Werner Design
Werks, Inc.

Principal: Sharon Werner
Year Founded: 1992
Size of Firm: 3
Key Clients:
Bloomingdales, Chronicle
Books, College of Visual
Arts, Comedy Central,
fX Cable Network, Levi
Strauss & Co., Minnesota
Public Radio, MTV
Networks, Musicland Stores
Corp., Nickelodeon, Target
Stores, VH1 Networks.

126 North Third Street
Room 400
Minneapolis, MN 55401
612 338 2550

erner Design Werks Inc. uses visual language as the sole staple to sharpen the success of the firm. "Visual language accompanied with sound design speaks for itself," says Sharon Werner, a former senior designer at Duffy Design Group. Utilizing this tool allows Werner's team to fashion design solutions tailored specifically to suit each client without curbing its true art form. An identity system for CoVA, a small art college in St. Paul to the VH1 Awards book, Werner's team philosophy synthesizes business savvy and a keen sense of design—producing work that earns client's praise and international recognition. Awards and honors from Communication Arts, New York Art Directors, British Design and Art Direction, American Center for Design, Annual Report 100, and *I.D. Magazine* portfolio the firm's strengths in effective and innovative design. Works are included in *100 World's Best Posters* and are part of the permanent collection of *The Library of Congress, Victoria and Albert Museum* and the *Cooper-Hewitt Museum.*

above
The drop cap was taken from a photograph shot by Darrell Eager.
Designer, Sharon Werner.

left
Illustration part of Werner Design Werks identity.
Designer, Sharon Werner; illustrators, Werner and Lynn Schulte.

above
Self promotional poster in conjunction with three other businesses. Each side of the poster has an important message about communication.
Designers, Sharon Werner and Amy Quinliven; photography, Michael Crouser; copywriter, Amie Valentine.

left and opposite page
Identity system for Joanie Bernstein, an art representative out of Minneapolis, MN. To create an identity that doesn't overpower the illustrators she represents, large type, mill end papers and low-tech printing were incorporated to create an inexpensive, but effective and powerful design..
Designer, Sharon Werner.

top left and right
Awards book for VH1, New York, NY. The sales piece was developed to create interest and sell air time for an awards show in the planning stages. Various details allowed the piece to be updated as more information became available. The goal was to make the viewer feel as if they had been let in on an exciting secret about to happen. Designers, Sharon Werner and Amy Quinliven; creative director, Cheri Dorr of VH1; photography, Paul Irmiter, Shawn Smith and Lizzie Himmel.

left
Illustrator's promos for Joanie Bernstein. The pieces show two very different illustrators represented by her—capturing the feeling of the artist's style while still maintaining a loose system and ongoing identity for Bernstein.
Designers, Sharon Werner and Sarah Nelson; illustrators, Dan Picasso and Eric Hanson; photography, Darrell Eager.

above
Honors book for VH1. The "Red Book" is the program guide to the Honors concert for artists who contribute to special organizations. Designed as a biography of the artists and their respective organization, it contained a dedication page, table of contents and picture plates. The back section of the book is an out-of-date, donated, damaged or unsalvagable library book on environmental or music-related topics from the basement of the Minneapolis Public Library; a globe in the back is protected and displayed like a jewel. Designer, Sharon Werner; creative director, Cheri Dorr of VH1; photography, Darrell Eager.

right
Watch for Nick at Nite, New York, NY. Used as a premium gift, as time flies by, the Nick at Nite Man points to the cable channel's slogan. Designer, Sharon Werner.

far right
Programming brochure for Nick at Nite, New York, NY. Video stills or other sources were used because the network shows re-runs, so often there are no images available. "We tried to make the most of the photos by playing around with cropping, outlining and juxtaposition," said Werner. "This direction actually fits with the overall concept of Nick at Nite, giving each program a distinct personality under the Nick at Nite umbrella." Designer/Illustrator, Sharon Werner.

below
Cookbook for Chronicle Books, San Francisco, CA. The writing portrays soup as a comfort food, so the design needed to reflect the concept. The use of the tomato-red color band and script type on the cover plays off familiar canned soup, allowing the book to be identified from across the store. The book's playfulness is kept to the more non-essential divider and intro pages, giving room for the recipes to be easily read. Designers, Sharon Werner and Sarah Nelson; creative director, Jill Jacobson of Chronicle Books; photography, Darrell Eager.

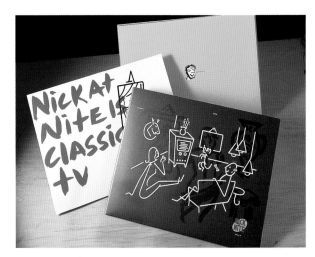

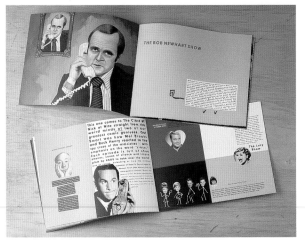

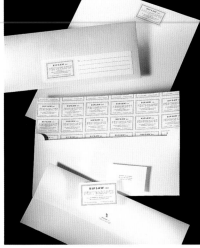

left
Identity and business paper system for Ripsaw Photography, Minneapolis, MN. Instead of using the literal image of a saw, it is indicated subtly, such as the perforation on the business cards and envelopes, and tooth-edged labels. Designer, Sharon Werner.

below left
Packaging system for textiles imported from Laos, by HMI Resouces, Taipei. To accent the scarves' beauty, the book tells of its history and how the scarves are made. The box is a sales kit sent to retail buyers. Designers, Sharon Werner and Sarah Nelson; copywriter, Jeff Mueller.

left and below right
Annual report for Musicland Stores, Minneapolis, MN. With concept stores such as Media Play, Suncoast Video, On Cue, as well as Musicland's financial status, the statement, driving concept and image of "It's not just Rock and Roll," is appropriate to communicate to the investor. Designers, Sharon Werner and Amy Quinliven; photography, Bill Phelps, Lizzie Himmel and Brandon Bathrick.

below
Archer Farms packaging for Target Stores, Minneapolis, MN, the store's commodity food products. The packaging is clean and versatile enough to fit with a variety of products, and have a familiarity to the consumer. Designers, Sharon Werner and Todd Bartz; creative director, Mike Thomas of Target Stores.

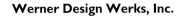

below
Poster advertising a lecture series that takes place each Tuesday in March for the AIGA, Minneapolis, MN. The front of the poster contains the most important information with more details on the reverse side. Designers, Sharon Werner and Sarah Nelson and photography, Darrell Eager.

right
Target Store's invitation for a meeting about packaging to reduce waste. "It is purposefully ugly and overpackaged to make a point," said Werner. "Most of the pieces were actually elements found in the back room at the stores." Designers, Sharon Werner and Sarah Nelson; creative director, Kim Hack of Target Stores.

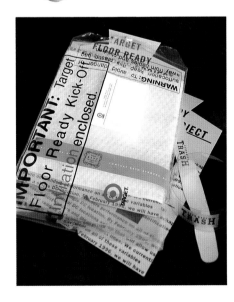

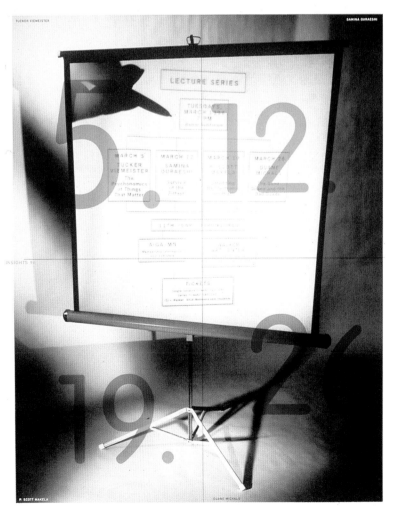

right
Promotion for Cliff Rakerd, Minneapolis, MN. As a voice talent/actor, the promotion played on his Boy Scout personality by creating a survival kit for potential employers... call on Cliff to solve any broadcast emergency. Cliff's name was also used as visual puns to make it more memorable. Designers, Sharon Werner and Sarah Nelson; copywriter, Jeff Mueller.

far right
Cookbook for Mick Freund, Minneapolis, MN. What every bachelor needs to survive in the kitchen. Helpful hints on how to prepare dinner for first dates (and how to gracefully end last dates). For the man who is an amateur in the kitchen but a professional in the shop. Try one of the handy tool-exchange suggestions: no mixer? Use a drill. Designer, Sharon Werner; copywriter, Lisa Pemrick.

left
Media kit for fX Networks, New York, NY. The programming is an eclectic mix of homespun shows—a collectables program and a breakfast show filmed out of the various rooms of a Manhattan apartment. A modern-day family scrapbook was created using the stuff on refrigerators, in junk drawers, and other small compartments to express daily life.
Designers, Sharon Werner and Sarah Nelson; creative director, Cheri Dorr of Melon; photography, Darrell Eager.

COLLEGE *of*
VISUAL ARTS

above
Identity system for College of Visual Arts, St. Paul, MN. The system reflects the school's long history of tradition with a focus on foundation studies. Designers, Sharon Werner and Sarah Nelson.

above
Media brochure for Comedy Central, New York, NY. The concept ties into the existing tagline, "What the Hell is Going on Here." Designers, Sharon Werner and Todd Bartz; creative director, Saul Torres of Comedy Central.

below left
Identity and application for Mystic Lake Casinos, Prior Lake, MN. "We saw this as an opportunity to educate the patrons of the casino on the culture and heritage of the Madewatekan tribal community," said Werner. "We worked closely with the tribe to learn about their traditions and heritage for the symbolic identity." Designer, Sharon Werner; creative director, Mike Murray of Hunt Murray.

below right
Identity system for copywriter, Rachel Eager, Minneapolis, MN. Old school supplies and doodlelike logo gives the feeling of her profession. The business card, designed like a composition book, allows her to give a sample of her writing with each card. Designers, Sharon Werner and Sarah Nelson; copywriter, Rachel Eager.

above
Popcorn and nut packaging for Deb's Delectable Delights, Minneapolis, MN. Targeted for upscale gourmet and gift shops, the packaging is a flat sheet that is folded and locked together around the product, making it stand up well on the shelf. Designer/Illustrator, Sharon Werner; copywriter, Charles Hanna; photography, Dave Bausman.

below
Identity and cassette tape for RadioActive Ink, Minneapolis, MN. To promote these two radio writers, silver-backed paper was the color theme with stickers that are hand applied to the letterhead, business cards and envelopes. Designer, Sharon Werner.

Words + Pictures for Business + Culture

Principals: P. Scott Makela, Laurie Haycock Makela
Year Founded: 1985
Size of Firm: 4
Key Clients: Arthur Andersen & Co., Deutsche Grammophon, Minneapolis College of Art & Design, Propaganda Films, Raygun Publishing, Sony, Warner Brothers Records, Vans Shoes, Walker Art Center.

Cranbrook Academy of Art
1221 North Woodward Ave.
Bloomfield Hills, MI 48303-0801
810 645 3083
www.grfn.org/~makela/

P. Scott Makela's Words + Pictures for Business + Culture, joined by soulmate Laurie Haycock Makela, began as an umbrella that encompassed what is called the "true media hybrid"—a modern genre determined to violate traditional structures of all mediums—from television, film, music and music videos, fashion, technology, typography, print, industrial design and sound. Originally based in Minneapolis, the firm recently moved to Michigan where Scott and Laurie happily took an Artists-in-Residence position at Cranbook Academy of Art. "As a married couple whose work and passions epitomize a new generation of designers, P. Scott Makela and Laurie Makela go out of their way to invade boundaries and twist the rules," wrote Mike Noble (*Graphis*, July, 1996). "The Makelas forge visual pathways for those designers inclined to follow their lead. By all indications, many are lining up to do just that."

above right
Paper promotion for Mohawk Paper Mills, Cohoes, NY. The multi-spread, text/image collaboration was fueled by industrial designer Tucker Veimiester's essay on the value of simply "do nothing" versus trying to constantly redesign and correct the mechanics and ecology of the world.
Designer, P. Scott Makela; writer, Tucker Viemiester; editor, Michael Beirut, Pentagram.

right
Cover for *How* magazine, F&W Publications, Cincinnati, OH. Assembled text from aged research documents on Haitian Voodoo, it acts as a rear stage to the levitating words in the foreground. The "Wild" is texture-mapped appropriately with the flesh of a human hand.
Designer, P. Scott Makela.

DEAD history

left
Laurie Haycock and
P. Scott Makela.

far right
Typeface for Emigre
Graphics, Sacremento, CA.
Distributed worldwide, "the
font is a hybrid of modernist
sensibilities merged with
the biomorphics of hand
lettering."
Designer, P. Scott Makela.

right
Book design for the Walker
Art Center, Minneapolis,
MN. For an exhibition that
traveled world-wide, *In the
Spirit of Fluxus* captured
the humor and irreverence
of the period.
Designers, Laurie Haycock
Makela and Mark Nelson;
"Carmela" typeface,
P. Scott Makela.

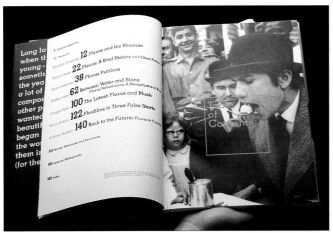

above
Front and back covers for
the The Minneapolis
College of Art & Design's
catalog, Minneapolis, MN.
After producing the previous "hyper-loud" 1991-93
version of the MCAD catalog, the school requested a
slightly lower "signal to
noise" ratio for its 1993-95
prospectus. The catalog
deliberately comprises the
digital building blocks as an
animation or film.
Designer, P. Scott Makela;
videography, Rik Sferra,
Alex Tylevich and Makela.

left
Book design for Walker
Art Center, Minneapolis,
MN. *Bruce Nauman* is a
monumental catalog of
over 400 pages. With an
ear on the cover and
words on the book's fore-edge, the formal typography
supports the artist's
"master" status and the
academic intentions of
the curators.
Designers, Laurie
Haycock Makela and
Kristen McDougall.

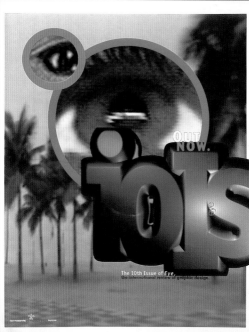

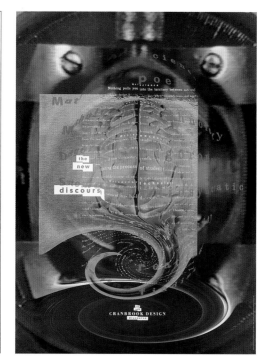

above
Conference poster for the American Center for Design, Chicago, IL. The merging of a muscular human neck, adult cable TV "scramble," and the Red, Green, Blue (RGB) balls define the surface territories and metaphors of new electronic media. Designer, P. Scott Makela; photography, Rik Sferra.

above center
Poster for the 10th anniversary issue of *Eye* magazine, London, England. The design magazine featured an interview with Makela. Designer, P. Scott Makela.

above right
Poster for the Cranbrook Academy of Art, Bloomfield Hills, MI and Rizzoli Publishing, New York, NY. "If it could visually be described, the centrifugal force of working/creating/purging in the Cranbrook design department at this endpoint of 10 years, the screaming orange brain in machine locks would be the picture." Designer, P. Scott Makela.

right
Poster and World Wide Web home page exhibited at Kendall College of Art & Design, Grand Rapids, MI. It demonstrates that birth and fire are linguistic inversions of each other. These images were composed to express the burning tongue of new language, meaning and digital form-making. Designer, P. Scott Makela; photography, Bill Phelps.

opposite page bottom
This series of books, published by the Getty Center for the History of Arts and Humanities, are editorially complex and detailed studies in historical typography for modern readers. Designer, Laurie Haycock Makela; series designed by, LHM and Lorraine Wild.

left
Music tour promotional poster for David Sylvian, Virgin Records, Los Angeles, CA. The Buddhist inspirations of the open heart define the spirit of the avant-garde musician's concert tour through Japan, the United States and Europe. Designers, P. Scott Makela and Laurie Haycock Makela; photography, Bill Phelps.

right
Corporate identity for Propaganda Films, New York/Los Angeles. "The well-known, far-reaching avant-garde film production company wanted a new symbol to represent its powers of persuasion and proletarian aesthetics." Designer, P. Scott Makela and Laurie Haycock Makela; photography, Bill Phelps.

below left
Portable work station for NYNEX Media Lab, New York, NY. The prototypical study for a portable work station challenged the expectations and fantasies for future personal computers. Interface design, P. Scott Makela; industrial design, Don Carr.

far left
Back and front covers for *Design Quarterly*, Walker Art Center/MIT Press, Mineappolis, MN. As the band-width of satellites, telephone and telecomputers expand, so does the potential for "close" and highly personal arrangements of digital information. An enclosed essay visualizes and describes the future data work space and idiosyncratic habits of a priest, plumber, auto mechanics and artist. Designer, P. Scott Makela; journal design, Laurie Haycock Makela.

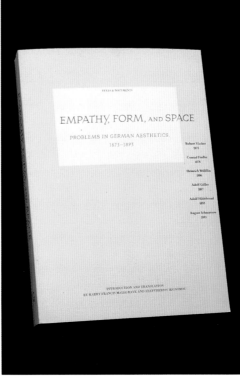

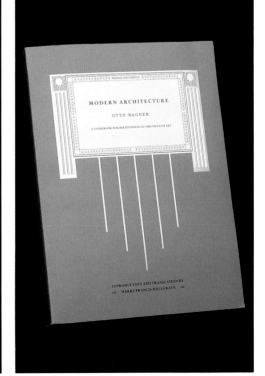

below
CD cover for Ray Charles, Warner Brothers Records, Los Angeles, CA. The limited release disc was controversial in that the placement of typography is over the blind singer's eyes. Designer, P. Scott Makela.

below middle
CD cover for musician/artist David Sylvian, Virgin Records. The cover shows a mother breast-feeding her child opposite an ocean invertebrate.
Designer, P. Scott Makela; photography, Bill Phelps.

right and below right
CD cover and packaging for AudioAfterBirth, Makela's industrial deep-soul music, Emigre Music, Sacremento, CA. The packaging employed a delicate black typographic band embracing a photograph of the birth of Carmela, his daughter. Designers, P. Scott Makela and Rudy Vanderlans.

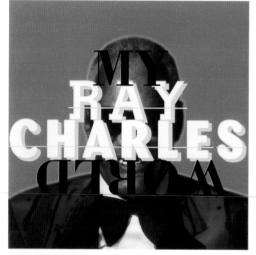

bottom left
CD cover for Todd Levin, Deutsche Grammophon, Hamburg, Germany. The musician's avant/classical compositions have a smart and dark edge, and reminded Makela of old detergent commercials around 1967. The simple italic blocks of typography indicate the parody of the "new and improved." Designer, P. Scott Makela and Rudy Vanderlans.

right
Television advertisement stills for Lotus Software Corporation. Merging Makela's atmospheric typography and Plansker's neo-dada imagery, this commercial spot for Lotus software offered an unexpected gestalt to software advertising.
Design Director, P. Scott Makela; director, Jeffery Plansker.

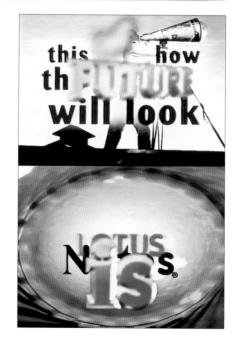

left
Music video stills from Michael and Janet Jackson's *ScreaM!*, Sony Music, Los Angeles, CA. The $7.5 million futuristic music video was shot in silvery black and white. Silicon Graphics animations and Elastic Reality technologies were used to create a science fiction aesthetic. Design Director, P. Scott Makela; video director, Mark Romanek.

bottom
Identity for The Walker Art Center, Minneapolis, MN. The Center's promotional materials are edgy and elegant, setting a precedent for the design of cultural institutions across the country. Design Director, Laurie Haycock Makela; senior designer, Matt Eller; designer, Santiago Piedrafita; projects manager, Michelle Piranio; intern, Deb Littlejohn; editor, Kathleen MacLean.

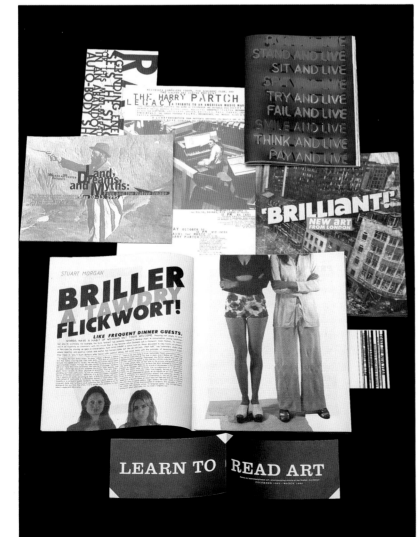

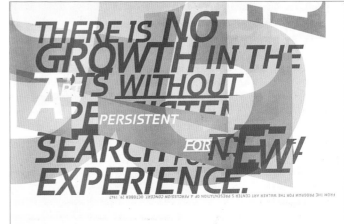